AFTER
THE
TRIP

UNPACKING YOUR
CROSSCULTURAL
EXPERIENCE

CORY TRENDA

Foreword by Tim Dearborn

≋
IVP Books

An imprint of InterVarsity Press
Downers Grove, Illinois

InterVarsity Press
P.O. Box 1400, Downers Grove, IL 60515-1426
ivpress.com
email@ivpress.com

InterVarsity Press® is the book-publishing division of InterVarsity Christian Fellowship/ USA®, a movement of students and faculty active on campus at hundreds of universities, colleges, and schools of nursing in the United States of America, and a member movement of the International Fellowship of Evangelical Students. For information about local and regional activities, visit intervarsity.org.

All Scripture quotations, unless otherwise indicated, are taken from The Holy Bible, New International Version®, NIV®. Copyright © 1973, 1978, 1984, 2011 by Biblica, Inc.™ Used by permission of Zondervan. All rights reserved worldwide. www.zondervan.com. The "NIV" and "New International Version" are trademarks registered in the United States Patent and Trademark Office by Biblica, Inc.™

While any stories in this book are true, some names and identifying information may have been changed to protect the privacy of individuals.

Cover design: David Fassett
Interior design: Jeanna Wiggins
Images: © tovovan / iStock / Getty Images Plus

ISBN 978-0-8308-4145-5 (print)
ISBN 978-0-8308-7405-7 (digital)

Printed in the United States of America ⊛

InterVarsity Press is committed to ecological stewardship and to the conservation of natural resources in all our operations. This book was printed using sustainably sourced paper.

Library of Congress Cataloging-in-Publication Data
Names: Trenda, Cory, 1954- author.
Title: After the trip : unpacking your crosscultural experience / Cory Trenda.
Description: Downers Grove : InterVarsity Press, 2018. | Includes
  bibliographical references.
Identifiers: LCCN 2018012249 (print) | LCCN 2018018282 (ebook) | ISBN
  9780830874057 (eBook) | ISBN 9780830841455 (pbk. : alk. paper)
Subjects: LCSH: Christianity and culture. | Travel--Religious
  aspects--Christianity.
Classification: LCC BR115.C8 (ebook) | LCC BR115.C8 T748 2018 (print) | DDC
  263/.041--dc23
LC record available at https://lccn.loc.gov/2018012249

P	20	19	18	17	16	15	14	13	12	11	10	9	8	7	6	5	4	3	2	1
Y	35	34	33	32	31	30	29	28	27	26	25	24	23	22	21	20	19	18

CONTENTS

Tim Dearborn

I talked with a recent returnee from his first short-term mission trip and once again heard the comment, "It changed my life." Two thoughts came immediately to my mind: "Praise God," and "I wonder how much change and for how long." Millions of crosscultural travel veterans attest to the frustrating truth that it takes more than a profound experience, strong memories, and good intentions to change our lives. The pressure to revert to life-as-before creates daunting barriers to the kind of transformation for which many long.

Yet we know that neither the people who supported our trip nor those who hosted us did so only for it to be one more interesting experience in our lives. As I wrote in *Short-Term Missions Workbook*, we are sent on these trips to grow from being merely "mission tourists" to becoming "global citizens."

Cory's ministry and now this book provide vital insights to lead us into global citizenship. Cory summarized the challenge he seeks to overcome: "You may be surprised—and disturbed—to learn that studies have almost universally found *no measurable long-term effect* of these encounters on the lives of trip participants!" It seems doubtful that many would want it to be this way, or that this would align with God's will.

There is a passion and sense of urgency behind Cory's writing. He's driven by the concern that two million Americans have significant crosscultural travel experiences each year, yet, as he wrote to me, "It's so discouraging to see not only wasted money and effort, but wasted opportunity."

To counter this, Cory develops a Christ-centered process for a lifelong journey that integrates the insights gained from crosscultural trips into our everyday lives. This book is a travel guide for the journey that begins once the trip is over. As we appropriate these insights, we can find wisdom to integrate seemingly incompatible life experiences into a radical love for God and all our neighbors—those who are next door, and those who live in remote and often precarious contexts, dangling over the abyss of poverty.

I have known Cory for almost thirty years, and during that time he has led hundreds of people on scores of vision trips—crosscultural mission trips that are carefully designed to expand our vision. Unlike most short-term mission trips, the focus is on what happens in our lives once we return home. The goal is that as a result of what and, more importantly, who we saw while traveling, we would see life, the world, people who are materially poor, God, ourselves, and maybe even our own vocations differently. Cory weaves together his vast experience from such trips with testimonies from participants, humility about his own foibles, humor, and engaging stories into this post-trip travel guide.

Cory opens us up to what I believe is God's goal for our crosscultural mission trips: "*We ourselves* become crosscultural." In so doing, we fall deeper in love with the world that God so loves. We are delivered from living in our own small hearts that are often painfully boundaried by fear, pride, and loneliness. We are transported further along on the journey of living in, from, and with the great heart of God.

1

It's the end of your crosscultural experience. You've picked up many memories and memorabilia, and along the way you've left pieces of yourself behind. You've given and received gifts and purchased more for family and friends.

On that last night before returning home, if you're like me, you aren't even sure anymore what's in your bag or suitcase, and you're fairly certain you can't take all of it with you. So you pull everything out and spread it on your bed or on the ground, and you try to sort it all out—what to take home, what to leave behind, what reminds you of important encounters, and what it all means. Maybe you brought a few "necessities" from home that you didn't need after all. Maybe a few things don't fit *you* very well anymore. And you are determined to make room for some new items that you want to have a part in your ongoing life.

In the same way, your heart and your mind will go through a similar sorting process as you wrap up your encounter, return home, unpack your bags, and resume your regular life. You will try to sort it all out, except that you know this is not a task you can complete in an hour or two. Or a day. Or a week.

In fact, if you truly want your experience to be life changing, you'll be sorting it and working it out for the rest of your life. After all, that's what *life* change means.

THE PATH TO LASTING CHANGE

Crosscultural encounters leave us with vivid memories, writing seemingly unforgettable stories on our brain with permanent ink.

But as time progresses, memories and good intentions fade when they aren't an active part of our life. Perhaps you're reading this only weeks after your trip, and you've already felt such a fading. So how do we move the memories from our head to our heart, and finally to our feet and hands? And what does it mean for a one-time crosscultural experience to be truly life changing?

In recent years there has been much consternation among mission and educational leaders concerning the actual value of mission and volunteer trips. You may be surprised—and disturbed— to learn that studies have almost universally found *no measurable long-term effect* of these encounters on the lives of trip participants!

Still, I'm confident that these experiences have the potential for great good for those who go. Of course, the key word here is *potential*, and much of that potential has to do with whether or not this once-upon-a-time experience actually becomes integrated into the participant's ongoing life.

People often fall into one of two traps after their crosscultural experiences. Some put a thick firewall between their home culture and the one they visited, and they do their best to not allow their trip experiences to seep into their cozy worldview. Conversely, others condemn everything about their home culture. Once they come back they make everyone around them miserable with judgmental statements about what others need to do differently because the traveler has now become the enlightened one.

But there is a third way. It's neither fast nor drastic. But it's the key to an experience that truly earns the label *life changing*. This third way is integration. Integrating, or interweaving, a one-time experience into your ongoing life means being thoughtful, a lifelong learner, someone who continues to seek ways to engage across cultures. Integration respectfully holds in tension differing worldviews or cultural realities and attempts to incorporate the best aspects from both, while also holding both up to the light of the gospel.

Integration is not theological syncretism. But as you no doubt have experienced, every culture is a mixed bag of strengths and weaknesses—including your own. *There is no human-made culture that is a perfect reflection of the coming kingdom of God culture* that Jesus spent his entire ministry describing. People from every culture that I have encountered have given me new glimpses of that soon and coming kingdom through their values, paradigms, and choices. These are the treasures I want to glean, the pieces of a culture that I wish to add into my own worldview, so that my ongoing life choices, attitudes, and actions might be closer to those of Jesus.

It takes time and honest effort to synthesize our experiences into actionable lessons that can, over time, actually change one's life trajectory. That's what this book is designed to help you do. I believe that this is exactly what God expects from us: to learn and integrate the best lessons from every human culture that God exposes us to, in order to live more like Jesus and reflect more of God's kingdom on earth.

I love people. I love seeing how they interact, what makes them happy, what they worry about and don't worry about, how they love and care for one another. And in this school of human nature, everyone can be my teacher—if I'll open myself to being taught.

It's an exciting journey, this journey of integration, where one-time encounters can alter us and become truly life changing. The Peace Corps handbook for returning volunteers states that their most successful returned volunteers "did not put their Peace Corps experience behind them. Instead, they took it with them and threaded it through their lives."

This "threading," or integration, takes time, patience, a posture of learning, ongoing engagement, and—*gulp!*—an openness to actually embracing change. Only a commitment to a larger, more God-honoring life can give us the courage and power to overcome our inertia and our fear of the unknown. But the good news is that, armed with this commitment and the principles on the following pages, you already possess your most important tools!

GETTING THE MOST OUT OF THIS BOOK

The upsurge of crosscultural mission-related travel—estimated at two million Americans each year—is quite a recent phenomenon. Hundreds of books, articles, and Bible studies exist to prepare travelers before and during their trips. But beyond a few tips for returning home tucked into the last chapter of a book you've now misplaced along the journey, very few resources exist for helping earnest travelers transform their one-time experiences into lifelong learning and change *after the trip*.

Many people want their trip to be life changing, and yet the trip in itself can't possibly be so! It's only as your post-trip life unfolds that this transformation can begin to come to pass. Therefore, your ongoing decisions *after you return home*—to either process or ignore, zone out or lean in—are crucial to whether your wish and hope and prayer for a life-changing experience comes true.

This book humbly attempts to aid you in that critical process of integration. Together we can also begin to change the currently condemning statistics about the *non*-impact of these trips on the ongoing lives of participants. I hope to share useful tips and proven principles as well as provide glimpses into my own attempts at interweaving my crosscultural encounters into my ongoing life.

Quotes from past trip participants and leaders are featured throughout. As part of the preparation for writing this book, I distributed two surveys: one for past trip participants and another for trip leaders. The respondents, representing numerous churches, denominations, and mission agencies from over a dozen US states, express feelings you've probably had and raise some important issues we'll be addressing in these pages. At the end of the book are "Questions for Reflection and Discussion" designed for group and personal reflection, plus an appendix featuring Tim Dearborn's Eight Great Questions to further help you process your reentry.

It's amazing to realize that we can actually glean a lifetime of learning from our one-time crosscultural experiences, and our attentiveness to those lessons is key to a trip truly becoming *life changing*. May this book be a useful tool as you continue your own journey of discovery and integration.

2

When I'm back home, it's as though I see God in black and white. But when I'm in Ethiopia, I see God in color. — BOB

The whole reason I'm in ministry was because of short-term mission experiences that opened up my worldview, so I know they can make a difference. I still think they can be a powerful tool, but . . . they aren't the Miracle-Gro of Christian discipleship! — MARK

You've probably heard an overly excited child ask their parent who has just returned from traveling, "What did you bring me?!" It's true that on our trips we often think about gifts we can bring home to loved ones and friends. But now turn the question around and ask yourself, *What did I bring* me? I'm not talking about the trinkets in your suitcase (although a few may represent important memories), but rather the invaluable encounters and experiences you've had. These are gifts—given by God, to you.

What does it mean to open these gifts? How do we assess their value to our ongoing lives, what to treasure in our hearts, and what to share with others?

SIGNALING A TURN

I was a little disappointed with myself that I did not come back with a life-changing experience. — **CHRISTINE**

When we return, we think we've changed. But the world around us has not changed, and we rapidly get pulled into prior routines and schedules of work, family, etc. Habits eat good intentions for breakfast. — **MARK**

You've returned from an encounter with the "other." You may have been in another culture, or another social or economic setting. You may have traveled across the border or halfway around the world. Or next door.

You may have gone to learn. Or to teach. Or to serve. To give or to receive.

You had amazing encounters with people very different from you and yet ultimately very much the same. You may have suddenly found yourself loving and caring about people and cultures that before your journey seemed alien and unattractive. You saw things that disturbed you deeply and experienced things that moved you greatly.

And now you are—or soon will be—back home, in a place that, in your quiet and more honest moments, suddenly may feel a little less like home.

Friends and family ask the obligatory question (and occasionally they actually want to know): "How was your trip?" You have experienced so many disparate feelings and thoughts that your head is in a jumble, and you search in vain for some short-hand summary that could encompass something so heart- and mind-expanding, because you couldn't possibly tell them everything.

"It was life changing!" you say with great seriousness, your head bobbing slowly up and down, eyes slightly squinted and thoughtful—all in a futile attempt to heighten your meaning beyond what your words can muster. It's not much, but it's the best you can do.

But later, you wonder what *life changing* really means, and whether your reply was anything more than a passionate hope that somehow your ongoing life might be different because of this experience. You *hope* the trip will not simply be a one-time memory that you line up on the mantelpiece of your mind beside images of your graduation day, the last time you saw Grandma before she died, your first kiss or first job or first child.

You go back to your regular life, because of course you have to—your work or school or church life. You buy things, you make decisions and judgments, and suddenly you find yourself making the very same choices based on the very same paradigms that you did before your supposedly life-changing experience. I've been there.

I cringe inside whenever I hear the term *life changing*. It means everything and it means nothing. *Thought provoking, paradigm challenging, mind expanding*—these terms are probably far more accurate. We've cheapened *life changing* by using it prematurely, before it can be infused with real meaning. And by claiming to have had the experience of lifelong transformation before it could possibly be true, we blur the line between reality and wish.

If you've been back a week, a month, or even a year, I would gently challenge you to articulate exactly how the experience has actually changed your life. Not only changed your thoughts but changed your actions and priorities: how you use your money, how you spend your time, how you pray, what you read, how you vote. And will these changes still be part of your life five or ten years from now?

Don't we all worry in the recesses of our hearts about whether there will be any lasting change in us *at all* from these experiences? As mentioned earlier, the vast majority of serious studies have shown no lasting measurable impact in the lives of crosscultural travelers and volunteers. None! If we are to be truly honest with our friends and families, we ought instead to come back from our encounters with other cultures and humbly say, "I hope and pray to God that my trip *becomes* life changing."

For an experience to fit that descriptor, there must be a noticeable alteration in one's future trajectory. Making a commitment to be a follower of Jesus ought to be life changing. Getting married is life changing. Becoming a parent for the first time is definitely life changing! These are not simply one-time experiences but rather the beginning of lifelong commitments. No serious married person or parent or Christ-follower can deny that these experiences bring with them major implications for how they spend their time, money, thoughts, and prayers.

You probably did not take your crosscultural trip in order to change your life to that same degree! But this book is a resource for people who don't want to forever remain the same, stuck in their former less-expanded, less-informed world.

Think about the GPS navigation system in a car. My GPS often can't discern when I've first begun to take an exit ramp and am no longer following the freeway. I have to create some distance between me and the road that I was barreling down previously before this change registers in the GPS.

The only way for me to tell that I've changed course is by seeing that I have actually altered my direction, not simply that I've activated my turn signal. It's not enough just to change lanes on the same freeway. I might slow down or speed up; I may turn on my flashers. But until I alter the course I'm driving, nothing has actually changed.

Similarly, life-change can only be measured after the fact. Only when we look back on the roads we have traveled and the places where we've turned are our previous course corrections made clear. Until then, we can only promise God and ourselves that we will not forget, we will not ignore, and we will try our best to learn from our experience and integrate its lessons into our life going forward.

Our desire to declare an experience life changing (albeit prematurely) is much like activating your turn signal. It's a sign that you *desire* to change course, that you *want* to move in a new way. And here's the good news: this desire itself is an offering to God, a measure of intent and even of progress.

Fitness coaches call this the "contemplation phase." At this point, I haven't increased my exercise or lost that weight yet, but I'm signaling that I want to. So being in the contemplation phase is a positive thing, or at least potentially positive. But it's also not the same thing as actually creating a fitness plan and then (yikes!) executing the plan.

Let me make one thing clear: your plans will evolve over time, and they will be unique to you, based on your experiences, the promptings you hear, and how you choose to listen and respond to them. There are no correct answers and no easy three-step methods for reflecting on and then integrating your experiences into your everyday life.

But in the pages that follow you will find some useful tools for leaning into your promptings, as well as some illustrations from my own encounters with the *other*—the poor, the foreign, the marginalized—and my struggles to integrate their lessons into my own life. My prayer is that God will use these to speak to you about your own experiences and invite you to discover your own hidden treasures. And if you traveled with a group, don't miss the chance to learn from each other and discover over time how others from your team are incorporating the experience into their lives.

Integration is a lifelong process—a habit, really, of openness. You won't finish it when you've finished this book. But consider this: through the journey you have already experienced, you've opened yourself up to God's invitation to a lifelong adventure.

You can choose to do what many travelers have done: simply file your trip memories away with all your past vacations, relegating it to a bucket list adventure, just another in our culture's never-ending infatuation with experiences. In the process, you will become another statistic—one that indicts mission travelers and accuses volunteer trips of having no lasting impact on the participants.

Or you can joyfully accept the invitation to growth, to seeing the world a bit more as God sees

YOU CAN'T POSSIBLY COME HOME WITH A LIFE-CHANGING EXPERIENCE BECAUSE YOU HAVEN'T HAD TIME TO CHANGE ANYTHING YET. BUT YOUR *DESIRE* TO SEE THIS TRANSFORMATION HAPPEN IS THE CRITICAL PRECURSOR TO IT BECOMING TRUE!

it, and to loving beyond your former limits, beyond anything you could ever have imagined.

I hope you'll activate your turn signal and begin the journey.

SAVE YOUR WORK!

I have been impacted by a story or experience and thought I would always remember it . . . but did not.   — ROBIN

It's easy to get back into your normal routine and forget about the experience— out of sight, out of mind.   — DANA

It wasn't long ago that a computer user could lose a great amount of work if they forgot to save it to their hard-drive memory every few minutes. Out of habit—and sweaty-palm experiences—I often remind myself: *Save your work!*

Our human memories are similar, and a critical first step to treasuring your experience and learning from it is to make an enduring record of it.

Some photos and a few faces are still etched in my mind, some for thirty-plus years. I'd like to say they are there forever, permanently burned on the screen of my brain. But I know better now.

In some darkened file folder I still have photos of my only visit to India, in 1984, and my first of many trips to Ethiopia, in 1986, shortly after the devastating drought and famine there wiped out an estimated one million souls. I flip through those photos from time to time and am ashamed at how little I remember about the vast majority—the names, the stories, why I chose to keep a certain photo with an "unforgettable" story behind it that I can no longer remember.

Memories fade. Important stuff gets lost.

I've damaged some photos by writing on the backs of them—names, stories, details—and others by adhering stickers with similar information. But at least those efforts help me remember and honor the experience and the people in the picture, which allows the memory to take me back, to move me once again.

Recently, my neighbor Brad told me that his father had served as an American paratrooper in World War II. Being half Native American and bearing a Germanic name, his father came under plenty of abuse. His dad died a few years ago, so Brad now possesses some unusual war memorabilia that his father collected during the conflict: lapel pins, cuff buttons, coins, and other small items that he took from each enemy soldier or civilian who was killed during combat with his unit.

His comrades-in-arms would get very angry, afraid that he might even go so far as to get into harm's way simply to "collect a souvenir." But for Brad's father, that wasn't the purpose at all. How could he explain it? His cultural heritage compelled him to carry a memento of each person to honor the sacredness of each unique human being, wartime enemies included, symbolically keeping something of that person's memory alive.

What an honorable extension of the spirit we ought to have when we encounter other cultures. It's about stewardship: the responsibility we have to treasure and esteem the people and encounters that God puts in our path.

My own methods have changed considerably over the years—from illegible journal entries scribbled onto a notepad to thumbs blazing across my smartphone. Someday soon this method too will be arcane. I've gone from having a few rolls of precious film to unlimited photos on a memory card, far more than I could ever remember the stories behind. We're diluting the very power of an iconic image by the sheer volume of them.

Photos, like Brad's collection of his father's war memorabilia, can contain deep stories within them. But Brad has no stories to make those items meaningful, no way to honor those casualties but for the silence of a button or a coin. A few exceptional photos need no words to have their effect. But you can be sure those are the rare exceptions. And in the quest for the perfect picture worth a thousand words, we can easily miss a personal connection with the human beings right in front of us, just beyond the camera lens. Let's be honest: a close-up photo of some nameless child or toothless elder is not a connection, just a nice picture no one else can comprehend and which you too will forget soon enough.

If you don't know the name and story behind the face in your photo, you missed an encounter. And if you do know those stories today, what could you do now to remember when you look at the photo in ten years? What do you passionately want *not to forget* ten years from now?

I find it is tremendously helpful to make a few daily notes along the way with names, quotes, and one or two key facts and then fill in the details during the journey home or within a week after returning. Also, through this editing and filling-in process I have wonderful ah-ha moments where the fragments in my brain connect and I more fully understand the meaning behind the experience. Equally important, a handful of powerful encounters from the trip that were jumbled up with all the others often seem to jump off the note pages, providing me the best way to share my experience with others.

That may not be your style, or you may not have journaled or made notes along the way. It's not too late to write about a few encounters that were the most meaningful. An exhaustive, day-by-day recounting of your experience is not nearly as useful to you—or others—as is thoughtfully capturing your most powerful encounters in a more permanent way. The sooner you can do this, the better—and not just for you, but also for those who ask about your experience.

How did you chronicle or create markers for your experiences as they were happening? What do you need to do now to solidify those memories, since they provide the very food for your journey of reflection and integration?

As Frederick Buechner writes, "It is precisely through these stories in all their particularity, as I have long believed and often said, that God makes himself known to each of us more powerfully and personally. If this is true, it means that to lose track of our stories is to be profoundly impoverished not only humanly but also spiritually."

When people in another culture give us the gift of their time, attention, and interactions, we owe them something back. There is a stewardship required. To whom much has been given, much is expected. Why did you see and hear and feel and touch what you did? Our experiences are not intended for hero-seeking "volun-tourism" or voyeurism. They are not for our entertainment or to leave precariously on the temp file on our brain's hard drive. They are for our transformation.

I believe that God gives us these experiences. And God invites us through these encounters to understand and love others more and to incorporate the lessons we can glean from them into our everyday lives. These encounters and lessons offer us an incredible opportunity to glimpse the world from God's vantage point: the God who sees and knows and loves the *other* every bit as much as we are seen and known and loved.

HONORING AND STEWARDING OUR ENCOUNTERS AS GIFTS—THIS IS WHAT NOTE TAKING, JOURNALING, AND REFLECTING ARE ALL ABOUT.

Can we believe that—that God and the universe want to tell us something, that our experiences are not accidental? Rather, they are gifts—gifts to be received, treasured, and remembered.

PICTURE WINDOWS

It's difficult to convey the significance of the journey in a succinct manner. I'd like to . . . clearly explain the trip and its impact without boring my listener to tears. I find it hard to convey the enormity of the experience in a way that helps the listener understand.
                                                                — CAM

These people and their stories are important. It's like once you know, you can't un-know them or their plight. So, I want to be a good steward of my experience.
                                                                — ANN

One person, one story, one life. Never underestimate the power of one.

Crosscultural experiences are chock-full of powerful moments—sights, smells, and situations that sear our minds. One of the most common feelings and statements during a trip is "Did all of that happen just *today?!*" Each day can seem like a week of experiences. Encapsulating all of these into something coherent when we get home is a near-impossible task.

I had this challenge after a one-week trip to Zambia. We were there to see several innovative poverty-alleviation programs and understand the context behind each one. It seemed a whirlwind; each day could fill multiple chapters in a book.

One morning we visited a health program. As we approached the humble clinic, we saw a long queue of mothers with their children waiting with weary patience to have their ill young ones screened. Sitting in the sun out front were those who had already been screened and still needed to see a health worker who could provide the drugs or treatments needed. A few steps away stood the HIV/AIDS clinic, where the staff provide testing and dispense life-saving antiretroviral drugs each month. We spoke with patients and volunteers, as well as the staff and attending physician. They were wonderful, sacrificial, even heroic people, many with names and stories I recorded, worthy of remembering, pondering, and retelling.

But our next encounter that same morning became my personal picture-window story from this entire trip. Our off-road vehicle bounced over increasingly bumpy paths into the bush, farther and farther from the main road, past an ox cart heaped impossibly high with hay, until we finally arrived at the home of Oswald and his mother.

Oswald was a shy, sweet ten-year-old and was clearly intimi-
dated by our group of strange-looking *mzungu* visitors. Like many
Zambian children, he was slight of build and small by Western
standards. (I'm always a bit shocked when I place my hand on an
impoverished child's arm or shoulder covered with their finest
second-hand American clothing, only to realize the skin-and-
bones frame underneath.)

Oswald had recently fallen sick, and we were there to hear his
story. Not knowing whether this was a serious illness or something
minor, his mother had been treating him with simple aspirin. It
would require *four hours* of walking to reach that health clinic we
had just visited. Personally, I resist driving my comfortable car to
an urgent care center only ten minutes from my home, where I
might have to wait half an hour to be treated. So I certainly can't
blame Oswald's mother—who was hoping her son would improve
on his own—for not wishing to make the arduous trek by foot with
a sick child in tow, then wait for hours in a queue just to be screened,
and then wait again if he was approved to be treated.

Thankfully, Oswald lives in a village with a community health
volunteer. Betsy is a buoyant woman who was tapped by her community as the first line of defense regarding health issues, especially for children. She had recently been trained and equipped
with a mobile health phone, a basic cell phone with a diagnostic
app that can be used by volunteers without advanced training. By
looking at the diagrams on the phone and pressing the right
numbers on the keypad, the volunteer proceeds through a series of
diagnostic questions via computer-generated text messages. The

mHealth app can help determine whether a child has a common illness or may have a life-threatening case of cerebral malaria. Then the app will automatically notify the nearest health clinic and make a priority reservation so the child can get a malaria rapid diagnostic test and get treated quickly.

Oswald's mother told us, "I don't know how it works, but Betsy took a cell phone out of her bag and pushed some buttons and asked us some questions. Then she told me, 'You need to take Oswald to the clinic!' So we woke up early the next morning and walked to the clinic, and when we arrived we did not even have to wait in the long queue to get prescreened. We got right in to see the health worker, and Oswald was tested and got his medicines!"

By the time our team met Oswald, he was fully recovered, and he told us sheepishly that he wants to grow up to become a doctor!

I love telling that story back home because it takes the rather technical concept of mobile health, which is hard to picture in one's mind, and focuses instead on impact, on saving lives—*one* life, possibly Oswald's life.

Josef Stalin infamously said that a million deaths is a statistic, but a single death is a tragedy. By the same token, a single life often provides the most powerful window into the plights and realities of many.

If someone asks me about my trip to Zambia or about health programs, I often tell them the story of Oswald. It illustrates poverty and malaria and captures the imagination regarding some new solutions that my listener and I can both be involved with, and it does all this through the lens of one child's story.

Here's the thing: we each need a clear window into the thousand unique experiences and lessons and realities we encounter on our crosscultural trips. Optimally, this window should focus on an encounter with a person or group that you can't get out of your mind. Their story provides a singular glimpse into the reality, challenges, or mindset in which many others also live, and so this story of one (one person, one group, one community—hopefully with a name you remember and wrote down) becomes the story of many.

Our friends and loved ones need that same window from us. You'll be asked many times, "How was your trip?" What I've learned through trial and lots of error is to answer by telling just one or two stories of specific people. Everything else you say is quickly forgotten; the stories are what will paint the picture. The faces and names and encounters that were powerful to you become the window for others to also see your trip. Add a pinch of spice, like climbing Mayan ruins or sweating through all your clothes, and you've got a recipe for doing what very few people do effectively: opening a picture window onto an overwhelming experience in the amount of time people are actually prepared to dedicate to your answer—usually a couple of minutes.

In these casual conversations, don't struggle to summarize the entire sweep of your experience with a slideshow or pithy top-ten list that will become a soon-forgotten curiosity to listeners, who may secretly wish they hadn't asked. In one sentence tell them the purpose of your trip, and then shift from the general to the specific: "And one of my most powerful experiences was . . ."

Who can't you quit thinking about from your crosscultural experience? What encounter keeps popping into your mind? Why? What emotions does that memory bring up in you, whether positive or difficult? How could you effectively tell this person's story, building a mental bridge over the aspects your listeners might not comprehend?

Here's a tip: people relate best to people, so telling a story of a person is more effective than simply talking about a program. And a person's story—such as Oswald's—prompts follow-up questions from your listeners, inviting further discussion as your answers fill in more of the surrounding context. "Tell me more about malaria. How do those community health volunteers like Betsy get trained? What's a health center in rural Zambia like?"

A picture-window story also helps you personally lock in an overriding memory from your experience that will become pearlized. Like the grain of sand in a clam's mouth that keeps getting worked over, the more times I've had Oswald's face in my mind and his story in my mouth, the smoother it becomes to tell. And in answering those follow-up questions, you'll discover key lessons you didn't even realize you acquired, further connecting the dots in your own mind.

The most important thing about your crosscultural experience was not the food you ate or where you slept or the

THE ONLY WAY TO EAT AN ELEPHANT IS ONE BITE AT A TIME. SHARING YOUR CROSSCULTURAL EXPERIENCE WITH OTHERS MAY FEEL LIKE A DAUNTING TASK. SO TAKE IT ONE BITE AT A TIME: START BY CHEWING ON ONE PICTURE-WINDOW STORY.

weather conditions. So don't force people to ask obtuse questions like those that may frustrate you both simply because you have not given them a more meaningful handle for grasping your trip. Telling your single story in two to three minutes might stimulate their thinking and help them know what other questions they could ask. Your picture-window story directs the conversation toward meaningful dialogue that can help both of you process and grow.

DEALINGS WITH FEELINGS

I haven't unpacked my suitcase yet, because I know that when I do I'll have to start processing my trip. And I'm not ready for that yet!   — RENE

One thing I brought back that I didn't anticipate was the emotional struggle. One particular challenge has been processing the experience . . . coming home to an environment where everything is status quo, meanwhile inside my heart was shattered in millions of pieces and I was left feeling guilty, depressed, and lacked the group support locally.   — JENNIFER

It's normal to have lots of tough emotions after an intense crosscultural journey, even a very positive one. Dealing with these feelings can require time and effort. It may even require extending forgiveness, to others as well as yourself.

Processing these experiences requires making some time for it and also giving it some time. You can't decide when the processing will begin and end. But by dealing with your feelings as they arise, you will uncover a rich vein of gold that you can mine for a lifetime, becoming more valuable as you dig deeper.

You'll help yourself by employing practices already touched on: journaling and proactively reflecting on experiences as they rise to your conscious mind. Even looking back through your photos can allow you to reassess, remember, and reorient.

When we don't attend to our emotional needs directly, they can come out indirectly through our actions, something we all know too well as "acting out." Finding yourself angry, diving headlong into work and life back home, sleeping excessively, having a spending spree, going crazy with your friends—all these and dozens more are ways we act out the inner feelings we haven't taken time to bring into the open and face head-on.

Processing these initial feelings isn't a chore to be set aside for the perfect opportunity when you can take a week-long retreat, ideal as that sounds! *It's already happening inside you.* By the time we begin to say our goodbyes and prepare to travel home, our hearts and minds are trying to sort out and understand what we've experienced, what it meant, and what to do about it.

Here's part of a journal entry I wrote after the same trip to Zambia where I met Oswald. The feelings and reactions I was dealing with might surprise you. And you'll also see how journaling about it helped me process the feelings behind my actions and attitudes.

········

I've been increasingly crabby since returning from Zambia this week, and today I realized that I needed to get in touch with the underlying feelings.

In a word, I feel anger, though anger no doubt masks other, deeper feelings. I'm mad at myself. I spent a couple hundred dollars on things for myself on my first day home! Why in the world would I come back from being with the desperately poor and go spend money on myself?

So now, I'm taking a few hours alone to reflect on my trip and simply be quiet. I'm sitting on a hillside that overlooks a peaceful canyon down below with rambling brush, crowing roosters, and disordered beauty. In contrast, just behind me are the well-ordered streets of my suburban town, with its clean curbs and carefully manicured gardens.

It strikes me that this little contrast—with me stuck right between the two realities—is a picture of what I'm experiencing inside at this very moment. Having just been in the midst of rural poverty and rugged beauty, I'm now expected to quickly process and articulate that experience in some understandable fashion for the benefit of the people quite literally behind me, the people who live like I live. Though this is who I've chosen to live among, still the impoverished rural poor of Zambia call to me.

This trip took more out of me emotionally than I expected. I can't seem to sustain my energy for more than a couple of hours at a time. A friend asked earlier: "Are you fatigued? Depressed?"

How should I know? Yes! But why should I feel depressed? I've just reviewed my photos and trip notes this morning. I didn't discover some dark memory I'd repressed. Instead, there was a bounty of happy faces, hopefulness . . . though perhaps less than we think we see on the surface through our eager eyes.

Maybe it's a feeling that the progress we saw in Zambia, while very real, seems so paltry in comparison to the gaping chasm between their lives there and my life here. The mobile health program we saw may have saved young Oswald's life. But that doesn't negate the fact that his mother still had to walk to get him to the health center—for four hours! Thanks to mHealth, Betsy may have convinced her to make the arduous trek, but she still had to make it, and so did her very sick young son with a life-threatening form of malaria that not one single child dies from here in America.

I know better than to compare the reality of rural Zambians to the reality of a suburban American like me, and I counsel other travelers against it all the time. And yet, being in their reality one day and back home in my own reality the very next day, it's hard not to feel some culture shock at the difference. In fact, shock is probably the only healthy response, on some level.

But as a result, all of the progress we celebrated last week as major improvements in the lives of the rural poor almost seem like a sick and twisted joke now, a mockery compared to the gap that still exists between our lives.

I think I'm on to something here, in terms of understanding my feelings . . .

Some people come back from these trips exclusively focused on the joy exhibited by some of the impoverished people they meet. "They might be poor, but they're happy!" is the general refrain, and they conveniently wash their hands of any need to care about nettlesome trivialities like sky-high infant mortality rates or terrible water-borne diseases. But this response is simply a reaction to being overwhelmed by the size of the need, and therefore they create some justification for not doing anything about it. It comes from feelings of futility: "I can't fix global poverty, so why be involved at all?"

Yet my feelings today and my recent spending spree are simply another form of responding to what is overwhelming. In my case, I'm overwhelmed at the gap between us. And my response is no healthier than those who deny the reality of extreme poverty and recoil from it.

But this is an impossible way for me to live, and an unfair way to measure people. Would I make fun of my two-year-old grandson Laith because he cannot throw a baseball sixty feet? No, I would be thrilled the first time he threw a baseball even six feet! Why? Because I am recognizing Laith's reality and measuring how he has progressed, not comparing him against my own reality. Do I want to be bitterly disappointed because Laith can't come close to throwing a ball sixty feet? Or thrilled that he is throwing it six times farther than he could have thrown it a year ago? Viewed in the latter way, I can rejoice in his progress.

If I don't know the poor as individuals, if I don't see their determination and grit, if I don't take the time to respect where they've come from, this whole poverty alleviation endeavor can indeed feel very overwhelming.

But I *do* know these things. I've met the people. I spoke with Grace and Shupi and Betsy and Oswald and Michael and Alphonsias. And they stood up and looked us in the eyes.

They told us with clear pride about the progress they have made and the accomplishments they have achieved.

They are not without hope. They are not evaluating their progress against the measuring stick of my tidy first-world life and simply giving up. No, they are bound and determined to keep making progress, to make a better life for their children, to cut down the number of kids dying, to build safer homes and run successful businesses.

They were not looking for my pity, nor for my discouragement. In fact, quite the opposite. They were bragging! They were baring their teeth and flexing their muscles. They are brave, and they are bravely facing their future. In fact, their bravery and tenacity inspired me and our entire group. We learned from them, we laughed with them, we loved them.

So it's high time I quit measuring their progress by my own cultural yardstick. All I have to do is look behind *them*, not behind me, to celebrate how far they've progressed forward.

* * * * * * * * * *

Though I've made many trips, it's still important for me to pay attention to what my actions and reactions after a trip might be signaling about my underlying feelings—and then deal with those feelings directly.

Here's the good news: your own processing has *already* begun, whether you're reading this on the journey home or your crosscultural experience was long ago. You can't keep it all locked up in your suitcase full of souvenirs and dirty laundry, and if you ignore your emotions, they will demand attention through your actions.

Have you caught yourself acting out somehow since you returned, or doing things that surprised or frustrated you? What do you think you were reacting to? How might you get in touch with the underlying feelings? Do you need to forgive or ask forgiveness from anyone— yourself included?

If you haven't already made time, carve out some space to explore your feelings. Prayer, journaling, reading, and reflecting on Scripture in light of your experience (see the next chapter) are all tools I've found to be immensely helpful. Take a mini-retreat, whether an hour on a commuter train or a weekend away from home. Talk to others from your team, seek out your trip leader or people you respect who have taken similar trips, or walk and talk with your spouse or a trusted friend. You can be sure others have struggled or are struggling with similar issues, so don't lock yourself in a private dungeon. Finally, acknowledge your unlovely or unloving thoughts. Be honest, at least with yourself. As I experienced after that Zambia trip, until we write, speak, or otherwise acknowledge our inner feelings, they can drive our actions and thoughts in ways we don't even understand.

Other aspects of processing—such as putting all the pieces together, understanding the trip's impact on your ongoing life, and deciding how to make future trips even better—will take more time and will be addressed later in this book. They don't need to concern you at the moment.

First, take some time to sort out your disparate reactions and feelings and to navigate them successfully. (See "Questions for

Reflection and Discussion" for a useful exercise on identifying your feelings.) This is exactly the place where many get stuck and never progress. Overwhelmed by feelings they have not acknowledged and addressed directly, they instead

DEALING EFFECTIVELY WITH YOUR FEELINGS IS KEY TO ALLOWING YOUR CROSSCULTURAL EXPERIENCE TO ENTER INTO YOUR LIFE.

create simplistic narratives to justify detachment and disengagement from the people and issues they encountered. But, understood and dealt with, our emotions can become our deepest drivers for transformation—our own and the world's.

3

MINING FOR GOLD

[A] prerequisite for my life truly being changed is that my mindset needs to change. As with anyone who has grown up in suburban America, I have preconceived notions about far-away places and different cultures that help me keep their problems at a distance, so that I can mentally justify continuing to live my comfortable life.
— JOHN

Every crosscultural journey has its own lessons to be gleaned, every encounter its unique impact on our lives. And over time we will discover more and more treasure from our past crosscultural experience—if we remain open to its lessons.

Because integration is a journey, if we honestly want our encounters to shape us, we have to not only *make time* for processing but also *give it time*. Often memories or connections come to us on their own, when we're going about our day. Giving it time means paying attention when an experience involuntarily flashes back into your mind. Then you can set a reminder or appointment with yourself to make time to reflect on that memory. You need to mark the spot so you can dig later for the deeper nugget—and then actually follow through on the reminder!

Still, as every miner knows, digging and sifting can be hard work.

Over the past thirty-plus years, I've spent countless evenings and mornings with fellow travelers during our crosscultural trips debriefing our encounters from the prior day or week, not to mention the many subsequent conversations once we are home. Though the activities and discussions and locations vary greatly, the main takeaway themes that surface are quite consistent and similar.

Though there is some value in understanding the insights others have gleaned, your most enduring crosscultural lessons are those tied to your *own* experience—your encounters with others, hearing their stories firsthand, glimpsing their values, and observing their actions and choices.

Still, experience is only a beginning. Many people in our culture are experience gluttons. I have one acquaintance whose motivating goal is to visit one hundred different countries. This guy admires people who have reached the hundred-nation mark, looks for exotic trips to take to add more countries to his "collection," and spends significant amounts of money to reach this milestone. Yet in many ways he is one of the least culturally sensitive or curious people I know. In short, it seems his goal is to *go*, not to *grow*.

Growth or life change doesn't require that you go to more places and have more experiences. There are undiscovered treasures in the experiences you've *already* had, and mining those can uncover great riches.

So let's look first at some of the postures of processing, if you will. These are key attitudes you need in order to become receptive to the lessons of your experiences and allow them to truly speak to you.

Think about your spiritual journey. Every generation has discovered anew and passed down timeless spiritual practices, such as prayer, contemplation, and Communion. These practices have helped seekers and disciples throughout the centuries to draw closer to Christ, take their faith more seriously, and grow spiritually, even as they glean fresh insights for their own generation through these timeworn methods.

Similarly, there are proven practices that can help you glean your own unique lessons and foster a lifetime of learning and true life change from your crosscultural encounters. To develop the eyes of our global God, you can employ these attitudes or postures to pay closer attention and dig deeper.

READING THE BIBLE THROUGH THE EYES OF THE POOR

Most of our participants return immediately to their jobs/schools and have little time to process what they experienced/learned/how the Lord is inviting them to change. Debrief team meetings held weeks after returning from the trip are too little and too late for real life change.   — DEBORAH

How do we plumb the depths of what God had in mind for our crosscultural encounters? In addition to prayer and journaling, reflecting on Scripture in light of our crosscultural experience and, conversely, reflecting on our experience in light of Scripture can be powerful tools for mining precious gems.

At times, our reflections may be driven by emotional experiences as visceral as wrestling through the question, *How could a loving God allow people like those I just met to live in such miserable conditions?* The velocity and ferocity of the facts on the ground about poverty and inhumanity can peel the plaster right off our neatly crafted understanding of God. In those times, we may be tempted to turn our feelings of helplessness and dissonance into anger toward God, pointing an accusing finger heavenward as we wrestle with God's goodness or power or even existence.

At other times, you might desperately want to understand how people living in such conditions could appear to experience real joy or be unreasonably generous, despite their circumstances or suffering. *What do they have that I lack?* we wonder in our quieter moments.

Recently I spent some time in the Czech Republic, a land controlled during the past century by the Austria-Hungarian Empire, then overrun by Nazi Germany, and then for seventy years repressed by the Soviet Union. Wandering through the Museum of Communism in the Czech capital, Prague, and reflecting on their long years under the thumbs of stronger nations, I marveled at the resilience of the Czech people and their ability not only to survive but now to thrive. *Where did they find hope during all those years?* I pondered.

Contemplating our lived experiences such as these in light of our faith is an important part of theological reflection. Consider changing up your Bible-reading habits or the books and devotional materials you use in order to dig into these questions and to integrate your crosscultural experience more fully into your understanding of God and Scripture.

In our Western society, it's easy to fall into a mindset of God as our private deity whose main concern is helping us pick the right college or job or spouse. Once we've had experiences outside our own societal worldview, and perhaps gained a more God-sized view of the world, these interpretations of Scripture and understandings of the God of the universe may no longer seem sufficient. I have found that I sometimes need to alter my spiritual habits to further develop this new mindset and not fall back into my old, nearsighted patterns of seeing and thinking. Being "transformed by the renewing of your mind" (Romans 12:2) is not a one-time process but a continual invitation. *Fear not! If the crosscultural experiences we've had were superintended by God, then to mine that treasure for our transformation is the only obedient response we can make.*

One of the strongest barriers standing in the way of our opening ourselves to God's kingdom and our place in it is our preconditioned understanding of how to interpret Scripture. We can hold on so tightly to what we've been taught that it feels threatening to realize that sincere Jesus followers in other cultures read the very same Bible passages yet find quite different meanings than we do, and they notice other passages that we virtually skip over. A friend of mine once vociferously insisted that, unlike other people, he does not interpret Scripture, he simply reads "what's written on the page!" Anyone who says that has no awareness that we each come to the Bible with our own a priori worldview, our own cultural paradigms, and our own needs. Our understanding of God often shuts out anything that might uncomfortably challenge our own lifestyle, not to mention our tidy perceptions of God and of our place in the world.

A few years ago I discovered a monastery not too far from me. Because it is a working Benedictine cloister, the monks gather multiple times each day for the Liturgy of the Hours. Vespers is at 5:00 p.m.

daily, and occasionally I stop in for the twenty-minute observance. It almost exclusively features antiphonal singing of the Psalms in medieval plainsong, and we few bystanders are welcome to sing along. It's quite different to experience the Psalms in this ancient way, word by word and line by line in their completeness as musical compositions, as in fact they were written. At times the words present themselves in new and more powerful, even discomfiting, ways.

It was here, as I heard the words of the Psalms come out of my own mouth, that I vicariously felt within them the mourning of those billions around the world and throughout the centuries who hang all their mortal hopes on these very words. Standing in the shoes of the poor and the oppressed, of those who feel they are at the bottom of the heap, imagine how these words become promises, how they might leap off the page and into your heart:

> But you, God, see the trouble of the afflicted;
>> you consider their grief and take it in hand.
> The victims commit themselves to you;
>> you are the helper of the fatherless. (Psalm 10:14)

> "Because the poor are plundered and the needy groan,
>> I will now arise," says the LORD.
>> "I will protect them from those who malign them."
>>> (Psalm 12:5)

> The LORD works righteousness
>> and justice for all the oppressed. (Psalm 103:6)

He raises the poor from the dust
>   and lifts the needy from the ash heap. (Psalm 113:7)

I know that the LORD secures justice for the poor
>   and upholds the cause of the needy. (Psalm 140:12)

As it turns out, much of the Bible is written not only *about* the poor but *to* the poor—words of comfort, of justice from exploitation, of life in all its fullness. Mary's Magnificat (Luke 1:46-55), which is sung at the close of vespers each day, has been called one of the most subversive religious texts ever written. Her hopes for the Messiah were tied up not in personal salvation (as our majority culture's theology might have preferred it) but, uncomfortably, in societal transformation, political justice, and even redistribution of resources. If you didn't see that previously, try reading Mary's words of amazement and hope through the eyes of those you've now met and learned to love who are poor, marginalized, or living under occupation—as Mary was. How might *they* read the same text?

And Mary said:

"My soul glorifies the Lord
>   and my spirit rejoices in God my Savior,
for he has been mindful
>   of the humble state of his servant.
From now on all generations will call me blessed,
>   for the Mighty One has done great things for me—
>   holy is his name.

His mercy extends to those who fear him,

from generation to generation.

He has performed mighty deeds with his arm;

he has scattered those who are proud in their inmost

thoughts.

He has brought down rulers from their thrones

but has lifted up the humble.

He has filled the hungry with good things

but has sent the rich away empty.

He has helped his servant Israel,

remembering to be merciful

to Abraham and his descendants forever,

just as he promised our ancestors." (Luke 1:46-55)

When we try to read Scripture through the eyes of the poor and oppressed, especially those we have come to personally know and love, it becomes easy to see how each cultural and socioeconomic group brings its unique—and important—perspective to Scripture. If we believe that we all belong to the body of Christ, why would we assume that our own understanding of Scripture is the only acceptable and correct one, the complete and final one, or that *I and my culture* alone have been uniquely assigned by God to be the "eye of the body" that sees all that is to be seen in the Bible? (See 1 Corinthians 12:12-31.)

Any understanding of truth is influenced by the perspective of the one who seeks it. Church leader Wesley Granberg-Michaelson purports that scripture's consistent portrayal of the "truth" about any social order is seen through the eyes of the poor and the marginalized. The Bible has that bias, and it was embraced by Jesus. He interpreted the truth about his society by focusing on the Samaritan, the widow, the oppressed servant, the outcast person with leprosy, the paralytic—all those whom the respectable, self-righteous leaders of society pushed to the margins and excluded. This way of seeing the truth of society from the perspective of the powerless and oppressed stands in contradiction to the version of "truth" seen from the perspective of rulers.

For those of us living in the wealthier nations of the world, the sooner we recognize that taking the perspective of the marginalized does not come naturally to us, the quicker we can adjust our tinted glasses and look again with more clarity.

These days, the drumbeat I hear in Scripture is God's passionate compassion for the poor, the orphan, and the widow. It catches me in the oddest moments: while chanting that day's psalms, reading those ever-troublesome Gospel words in red lettering, and even while slogging through the Law and the Prophets.

And when I pause and actually seek to understand the words there, rather than recoil as from a guilt-inducing scold or dismiss them as mere figures of speech as I was so often taught to do in my rich-world culture, I begin to understand this as the plaintive cry of the heart emanating from the lived reality of the biblical writer and his or her people, the cry of the marginalized. And I can quickly choke up.

If you feel dissonance between the biblical interpretations that you brought with you on your trip and the feelings or thoughts you've had during your journey or since then, consider this an exciting invitation to go deeper. Do not be afraid! Confusion is often necessary for growth. Disorientation allows reorientation, so embrace it as God's transforming process.

Consider widening your devotional reading to include spiritual guidance from other nations, eras, and ethnic backgrounds. The breadth and depth of Christian experience and understanding from around the world and throughout the centuries will deepen your understanding of others' perspectives and fuel your own faith journey.

Contemplative theologian Richard Rohr states, "In my experience, healthily vulnerable people use every occasion to expand, change, and grow. Yet it is a risky position to live undefended, in a kind of constant openness to the other. . . . Spirit-led people never stop growing and changing." May we never stop asking questions and never be afraid of changing our minds. Through my exposures to other cultures, my faith journey has been deeply enriched, my opinions and understandings have shifted, and I see things in multicolor that I formerly could see only in black and white.

Think of this: God knew beforehand everything you would see and experience. Each person you've only recently met has been known and loved by God since the day they were conceived, and God was already present with them long before you got there. God weeps with those who weep and rejoices with those who rejoice.

That includes the people you met, and it also includes you. None of your thoughts, explorations, or questionings will surprise or offend God.

Emmanuel—God is with us!

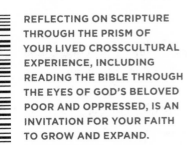

REFLECTING ON SCRIPTURE THROUGH THE PRISM OF YOUR LIVED CROSSCULTURAL EXPERIENCE, INCLUDING READING THE BIBLE THROUGH THE EYES OF GOD'S BELOVED POOR AND OPPRESSED, IS AN INVITATION FOR YOUR FAITH TO GROW AND EXPAND.

So use Scripture to discover the depth of the invitation the Holy Spirit has for you in your crosscultural experience and to better understand the God of the universe and how you fit into God's world.

YOU'RE NOT THE HERO OF THE STORY!

I need to humbly rein in my imago zoro *(superhero persona) and come back to Jesus' approach and teaching.*   — CLEO

When we return home, it's not uncommon for friends and family who didn't make the same journey to treat us like some admixture of Indiana Jones, Mother Teresa, the Crocodile Hunter, and Billy Graham. But you and I know better. It's important to put whatever service you may have provided during your trip into its proper context. Otherwise, circumstances may force a humbling reevaluation.

That's what happened to me while traveling in Afar, Ethiopia—an area as remote as it sounds. Our group took a Sunday afternoon outing to a nearby lake. Afterward, as we walked up a hot, dusty trail to get back to our vehicle, we saw six Afari men standing nearby. We had just heard that a sick woman had been carried across the lake on a makeshift raft. As we got closer, we saw the young woman lying under the shade of a tree, ill and still, on a woven mat with two heavy poles protruding from the ends. These six men had carried her all the way to the lake on this makeshift stretcher and then managed to ferry her across. Yet they were still twenty miles from the only clinic where she could get help that day, with no way to reach it before it would close.

We talked with the local staff who were hosting us: "Is there anything we can do?" They told us ominously that some time ago, staff had given a ride to someone who was sick with hepatitis. Soon everyone who had been in that vehicle developed hepatitis and was unable to do their important work for many days. So this was not something to consider lightly!

But because of this woman's obvious need (and my equally obvious consternation, I suppose), the decision was made for a couple of the local staff and me to risk driving her and two of her carriers to the clinic. They all insisted that I sit up front, however, farther from the sick woman. Meanwhile, her other attendants had to simply follow on foot.

We drove to the clinic, each lost in our own thoughts—no doubt praying for our personal protection along the way as well. Eventually, we all prayed together for God's healing for this Muslim woman, now limp against her husband's shoulder.

Then it happened: for a fleeting moment, I silently conducted my own award ceremony and pinned a little badge of pride on my chest for what we were doing and how I'd helped organize it. In my mind's eye, I even saw myself telling friends back home how we had served—and maybe even saved—this woman, despite the cost and risk to ourselves.

Immediately I found myself choking back sobs. *What did I know of the cost of servanthood?* These six Afari men, amid their harsh reality, had carried this sick woman *on a mat*, by hand and foot, fully expecting to walk the entire journey, until God blessed their team with our divinely orchestrated transport. Our little shuttle service was nothing compared to their service—days and miles of toil and risk, willingly undertaken on her behalf.

I had missed the point completely. King David had it right when he refused to offer a sacrifice that didn't cost him anything; the real value of any offering made to God is in direct proportion to the price paid by the giver (2 Samuel 24:24).

I took off my imaginary badge, repented, and gazed straight ahead from behind the pools in my eyes. I reflected on these Afari men, servants of Allah, and their example of costly sacrifice, ashamed at how much I still had to learn.

Pedestals are precarious. Don't wait for reality checks like mine, or for someone or some event to knock you off your imaginary perch.

NO MATTER HOW MUCH OTHERS MAY WISH TO HOLD US UP AS MODELS OF SELFLESSNESS OR BRAVERY, WE KNOW BETTER. WE ARE NOT HEROES. AND WE CAN'T LEARN FROM OTHERS WHEN WE ARE PERCHED ON A PRETEND, PRETENTIOUS PEDESTAL.

A posture of humility is a prerequisite to learning from others.

Let's be honest: what you and I "accomplish" for the kingdom of God on our trips is barely worthy of a footnote. We are not the hero of the story! And the sooner we recognize that—and disabuse others of any notions to the contrary—the sooner we can focus on the people we met, *their* sacrifice or courage or tenacity or graciousness, and the life lessons we can learn from them.

SEEK FIRST TO UNDERSTAND

It's frustrating to observe myself making snap judgments about people instead of seeking to understand them. But too often, in my rush to label who or what is good or bad or weird or awesome, I don't make the effort to first understand others.

Not every crosscultural encounter is planned, nor is it necessarily in another country. A few years ago, while attending a conference at a Midwestern hotel, I was exposed to a subculture of people I'd never known about: self-named Furries, who dress as animals. I came to learn that this is referred to as "anthropomorphic art," portraying animals as having human characteristics. (Think of shaking hands with Mickey Mouse at Disneyland.)

Imagine seeing random people walk around a business hotel lobby in normal clothing—but with an outsized raccoon tail following behind, for instance. The Furries were having their own convention in the same hotel, and I found it easy to purse my lips and knowingly raise my eyebrows along with my fellow conference attendees when we would walk past people in these costumes, though they were always polite and kind in their exchanges with us.

On our final night, the organizer for my conference apologized that Tera, his most valued employee, wasn't present. To make some point I no longer remember, he went on to tell us that Tera's childhood had been extremely traumatic, and she had suffered from depression and low self-esteem. But after high school she had discovered dramatic acting. As she portrayed various stage characters, she was required to exude qualities such as persistence, kindness, compassion, and courage—characteristics that Tera felt she lacked. Yet in acting she discovered new inner strength by taking these characters' qualities into herself and learning from them, and she gradually became a stronger person. It was a fascinating story. The organizer summed up, "If Tera were here, she would tell you that playing those characters saved her life."

Suddenly it hit me: God had prompted that story to be told. This was precisely the understanding I should have had toward the Furries. I didn't know anything about their personal stories or about the meaning this gathering might have for them. For all I know, donning the costume of a gentle woodland creature might have the same transformative impact for some of them that stage acting had on Tera.

The next morning before I traveled home, I sought out and had excellent discussions with several of the FurCon attendees and organizers. I have no interest in joining their ranks, but I came away with a greater understanding of their motivations and an appreciation of our shared human needs and desires.

Because I hadn't been anticipating a crosscultural encounter while attending a business conference, I hadn't prepared myself. Instead, I fell into the old habit of "judge first, ask questions later." But breaking old habits like snap judgments is part of being transformed.

We who have journeyed crossculturally should be the most curious, understanding, and accommodating of those who are somehow different from us. I know this, and yet so often it's only after I've learned a lesson and then catch myself once again acting like the old me that the most powerful learning is actually driven home.

IT'S NEVER TOO LATE TO SEEK UNDERSTANDING, AND IT'S ALMOST ALWAYS TOO EARLY TO JUDGE.

GET BEYOND IDEALIZING OR VILLAINIZING ANY CULTURE, INCLUDING YOUR OWN

I think a lot about our first day. We were crossing a bridge over a peaceful stream. . . . [Then] I looked down and saw a boy playing in the muddy water below, while another boy was drinking from it, one was washing in it, and another one was peeing into it, all within a few yards of each other. That said it all. — EMMY

As mentioned above, it's easy to experience another culture and slap a simplistic "good" or "bad" label on it. In fact, it can be downright satisfying emotionally. But such sweeping generalities, romanticized impressions, or blanket condemnations keep us from any real learning. Instead, it's important to recognize and acknowledge both the strengths and the weaknesses of any human culture. When we oversimplify a culture, we miss its subtle hues and the deeper insights hidden in its tints.

I traveled to rural Bangladesh many years ago, so I was pleased recently to present a friend with a watercolor drawing created by a Bangladeshi child. It was a lovely depiction of what appeared to be a peaceful scene from a rural village, perhaps the child's own.

My friend Jim and I admired it together, thinking about this predominantly Muslim nation and wondering about the images depicted in the idyllic scene: a young couple sitting on the ground

Figure 1. Child's drawing from Bangladesh

in marriage attire, a child near a small hut, and what seemed to be a church right smack in the center. Jim pondered, "I wonder what the words on the signs say?" So I emailed a colleague in Bangladesh to find out. The reply I received sent my mind spinning.

Dear Brother,

Greetings from Bangladesh. I am very happy and honored to illustrate the artwork. Please, find it as follows:

1. We see a man is exploiting a woman in the drawing (bottom left). This is one of the social issues by which the life of the children is affected much. The wording says, "Stop repression on women."

2. Now let's point to the corner where a boy and a girl are in bride and bridegroom dress. This is another social issue in Bangladesh that affects the lives of children. Early marriage/child marriage is very common in rural areas, especially in poor families who consider their daughters merely burdens. We have programs to empower the children in most vulnerable situations to combat the issues. They are working to stop early marriage through Child Forums. The little child [lower right edge] with a card represents the Child Forum's participation in community development activities. The wording means . . . "Stop Child Marriage."

3. Yes, there is a church in the middle of the village. . . . We have church in a Christian village. I think the child wants to say about his/her dream for the future . . . he/she wants to tell us about a society where there will be no "repression on women" . . . where there will be no "early marriage." . . . Finally, maybe it finds its expression in Kingdom of God values where there will be fullness of life . . . love and dignity.

I'd had an idealized interpretation of the artwork, very pastoral, peaceful, and pleasant. Now in the midst of this scene there was also ominous drama, especially when one remembers this drawing was made by a *child*—a child surrounded by the very real dangers from those issues. Imagine a child living in a harsh inner city, writing a poem about the violence around her: only the uninitiated who didn't speak the language would revel merely in its rhyme and cadence, missing its message completely.

Clearly Jim and I were the uninitiated here, not aware of the more nuanced reality. Now we have a both lovely and disturbing reminder of that child's reality, as well as perhaps a glimpse of the artist's childlike hopes for the peaceable kingdom.

All human cultures are a mixed bag, our own included. Today I took a break from writing and visited a county museum in the American South, near where we're staying while I write. Inside I turned a corner to find my wife and was stopped by her frozen face and red eyes. She was staring speechlessly at a display of a silken Ku Klux Klan shroud, and behind it a cross wrapped in pure white. The despoiling of this Christian symbol for the cause of white supremacy distressed and repulsed her and reminded us both of America's own checkered reality.

Beauty, injustice, triumph, heartache, menace, and joy are intermingled in every human-made culture. But the presence of one does not cancel out another. The beauty does not negate our responsibility to understand the trauma. And the trauma does not negate the need to appreciate the beauty.

One missions leader, Stephen, commented in his survey response on how crucial it is—both for us and for our friends from other cultures—to embrace complexity and avoid simplistic conclusions:

> If travelers can move into grief, pain, the dissonance of wealth and opportunity, and broken governments that stifle opportunity for the poor . . . if they can truly accept these realities, then their engagement won't be short-lived but based on a long-term engagement for change on both ends of the spectrum.

Simplistic assessments and judgments erode quickly and then wash away our connections to other cultures along with them. Look beneath the small glimpses you've experienced with people and their cultures. Ask questions when you return home. Reflect with nonjudging curiosity as to why family or community issues were handled the way they were. What prior experiences might these people have gone through that would inform their current practices? What do experts on the ground say?

For instance, the poorest people on earth generally live in remote rural areas, struggling to eke out an existence from the food they grow. Obviously, these farmers have the most to gain from improved farming practices. And yet the poorest people are the most risk averse. How frustrating this might be to volunteers trying to train them in modern methods! But why are these farmers so averse to trying new ideas? Because their margin for error is incredibly small: one failure could lead to destitution and even death. When those who want to help understand this, frustration can turn to empathy, and even to new ways of making progress, both through patience and through strategies that mitigate risk.

Lasting connection requires a clear-eyed understanding of the nuanced realities in which others live, along with a willingness to continue learning and adapting our understanding as time goes on. There is nothing useful in blanket judgments of good or bad. Worse, they allow for little

LET'S AVOID SIMPLISTIC JUDGMENTS. THERE ARE STRENGTHS WE CAN GLEAN FROM EVERY CULTURE, AND THERE ARE FLAWS TO BE RECOGNIZED IN EVERY ONE.

to no learning. We have to dig below the surface to find the real treasures beneath simplistic interpretations.

GRATITUDE IS NOT ENOUGH, THOUGH IT'S A GOOD PLACE TO START

We have since [our trip] been far more grateful for material blessings. . . . We have therefore been more conscious of helping those "least of these" we met in places like Uganda in our giving, and even our investing, using more of our retirement funds to help develop such nations.   — GARY

A friend sent me a note that might be similar to comments you've heard since returning home: "When you were in Africa a year or two ago, surely this thought came to your mind: *Thank God I am an American.*"

Gratitude is good. We are commanded in the Bible to always rejoice and be grateful (Philippians 4:4; Colossians 3:16; 1 Thessalonians 5:16-18, to name just a few examples). Yet the only record of Jesus himself giving this command is where he says to rejoice and be glad when we are persecuted and insulted because our actions are modeled after his (Matthew 5:11-12)! *Gratitude and action are to be inextricably linked.*

When I hear someone say that their primary response upon returning from a crosscultural encounter with those who are materially poor, persecuted, or otherwise disadvantaged is simply gratitude for what they have, I immediately think of the old saying, "There but for the grace of God go I." In other words, they are saying, *I have shoes. I have air conditioning. I have freedom. I'm so grateful that I don't have to live like those unlucky people we visited!*

I'm always rather astonished by that attitude. I don't recall Jesus' Sermon on the Mount including "Blessed are the *haves*, for they should be grateful." Or "Don't take it for granted when you are far removed from the suffering of the world. Rejoice, yes, again I say, rejoice!"

What happened to those bothersome injunctions to visit those in prison, weep with those who weep, comfort the sick—all those calls from Jesus to follow him in being incarnational and compassionate?

On the other hand, I recently had lunch with someone shortly after we both returned home from a crosscultural trip. As we settled into the upscale restaurant, she commented, "It's strange. Before our trip, I thought I'd feel guilty for all that I have when I got home. But I didn't feel guilty; instead, I felt grateful!"

But she seemed to have a different tone in her comment than many people do, and, fighting the instinct to pre-judge, I tried to probe her intentions more deeply. I came to understand that her gratitude was like that of Zacchaeus, whose response to encountering Jesus was to become uncommonly generous to others—a response that radiated out from his gratitude (see Luke 19:1-10). In a similar way, my fellow traveler was grateful to have the means to respond to what she had seen and experienced (which she promptly did, very generously).

A gratitude-induced response is far superior to a guilt-induced response. The latter is ultimately begrudging, something like paying a luxury tax for being one of those whom Ron Sider refers to in the title of his seminal book: *Rich Christians in an Age of Hunger*.

Successful real estate developer David Weekley articulates perfectly what my generous lunchmate felt:

No longer do I feel guilty for what I've been given; rather, I feel incredible gratitude that I am able to serve and to give. Out of that gratitude comes a deep sense of responsibility to use what has been entrusted to me in ways that honor the Giver of all gifts. When I act on that responsibility and give freely of my time, talent, and resources, I feel an awesome *joy*.

Did you catch the progression there? *Gratitude leads to generosity, and generosity leads to joy.*

Cicero, the ancient Roman orator, opined that gratitude "is not only the greatest, but is also the parent of all the other virtues." In other words, all virtuous action emanates from an attitude of gratitude. As it was for my lunch companion, gratitude can be the perfect place for us to start when we realize that we are fortunate to be in a position to give, to respond, to advocate—to somehow *act*.

No other response than action does any justice to our claims to be followers of Jesus, who was himself the consummate act-or.

When someone suggests being grateful for what you have as your best response to the suffering of others, find the words and energy to politely move beyond and improve on that notion, piling on more and better responses, responses of action.

Prayer is action. Learning is action (though indirect in itself, it can lead to wiser action and more informed prayer—as exemplified so well in Gary's quote that begins this section). Donating, being a voice and an advocate, directing investments toward social uplift, reviewing our lifestyle choices and their impact on the marginalized—these and other responses are far more germane, and humane, than mere gratitude. After all, we are blessed in order to be a blessing.

LET'S BE GRATEFUL, BUT GRATEFUL THAT WE HAVE NOW BEEN EXPOSED TO THE REALITIES OF OUR GLOBAL NEIGHBORS AND HAVE THE ABILITY TO DO SOMETHING ABOUT THEM. THEN LET US SEEK WAYS TO ACT INCARNATIONALLY, IN THE SPIRIT OF JESUS, OUT OF LOVE AND COMPASSION FOR OTHERS AND IN SOLIDARITY WITH THEIR SUFFERING.

Shortly after I wrote the preceding paragraphs, my seatmate on an airplane happened to be reading a newspaper article about the oppression of women in Pakistan and Afghanistan. I asked her about it, and she said, "It sure makes me grateful that I live in America, and that this wasn't the reality for *my* daughter."

The old frustration welled up in me a little bit, and I tried out my more expansive response, agreeing but not stopping at gratitude. "Yes, it does make me grateful, but it also makes me want to help the women and girls there and make a difference for them." We proceeded to have a cordial but circular discussion. My seatmate raised skepticism after skepticism indicating that these issues are unsolvable or beyond her control. What became clear was that she had truncated her circle of concern to only her local community. When she retires in a few years from her corporate leadership role, she wants to help youth in her area, because "we certainly have enough needs here."

Looking back, I wish I had said to her, "If the woman living in the house next to yours were being battered or oppressed by her husband, I can't imagine that you'd consider it a sufficient response to simply declare, 'As a woman, I'm sure glad I live in our home and not theirs!' I think you'd have to do something about it, something to help your neighbor.

"Further, if the police came to investigate a domestic homicide in that house and interviewed you, and you admitted to knowing all along about the escalating abuse but never addressed it, it would be considered scandalous. 'How could you know, yet do nothing?' the news and social media outlets would scream . . . and who would disagree?

"Responding to the needs of people who live farther away from us isn't any different. *Are they not also our neighbors?*"

Indeed; how can we know, yet simply be grateful for our own lot and do nothing about theirs?

4

TREASURES ON THE JOURNEY

Reflecting on Scripture, seeking to understand, embracing complexity, humility, and an inclination toward gratitude-inspired action—these are critical postures for effectively mining the treasures from your encounters. But what are these treasures?

I've gleaned many precious gems from my crosscultural encounters. But because the purpose of this book is not to prescribe the lessons you need to learn or even those I've learned but to assist you in discovering your own insights, let me simply provide two illustrations of how crosscultural experiences have helped me draw new realizations into my life. The first is an example of finding similarities between culturally different experiences and people and how these connections help me find common ground. The second illustrates how over time I continue to dig further for the underlying insights beneath an experience.

As you read, reflect on your own experiences. I think you may be surprised by how directly you can relate these examples to your own encounters. You may not have put your encounters into words yet, and perhaps this chapter will help you do just that—to reap your own lessons from your experiences.

The great news is that you don't have to take ten, twenty, or one hundred more trips to glean these insights or to have them influence your life. It's really a matter of choosing to look deeply into what you have experienced *already*, to mine the gold that has already been deposited in your heart and mind.

WE ARE MORE ALIKE THAN UNALIKE

For me, the first step was to internalize the truth that I have much in common with a smallholder farmer in Zambia. We share the same God, the same love of family, similar hopes and dreams.
— JOSH

The Poor are truly no different from us in their hopes and dreams and aspirations.
— BILL

One of the most moving aspects of our crosscultural encounters is discovering the universality of the human condition: parents' love for their children and desire for a better life for them, the bond of play among children everywhere, and feelings of compassion and empathy for those who are hurting or in greater need than we are ourselves.

These and many other universal human similarities provide transcendent bridges that connect us at the deepest levels to our fellow human beings—beyond our disparate cultural overlays. Maya Angelou wraps it up beautifully in her poem "Human Family":

I note the obvious differences
between each sort and type,
but we are more alike, my friends,
than we are unalike.

Or as Fr. Greg Boyle, founder of Homeboy Industries, which provides economic opportunities for inner-city youth and gang members in Los Angeles, has summed it up, "It's not us versus them; there is only us."

Around the world, people truly are more the same than their cultures are different. Sometimes this realization hits us when we observe someone from a very different culture responding with caring in the very same way as people we know from home. On separate trips to Africa, I saw women from dissimilar cultures show the same nurturing concern for children not their own.

In Malawi I met John and his two younger brothers, who were living together without an adult as both their parents had died. Their home was almost indescribable, no more than six feet by eight feet. The three boys slept on the bare dirt ground, with a blanket and a single peg for each boy's clothing being the only other articles I can recall seeing inside.

It was my first trip to an AIDS-ravaged region in those early days, and I felt overwhelmed and clueless. But one woman in our travel team, Kay, who was no doubt overwhelmed as well, funneled her feelings of disorientation and shock into a mother's compassion. She sat on the ground with the boys, she spoke tenderly to them, and with her words and countenance she showed them that they mattered. John, the oldest and therefore the one who always tried to be strong, furtively wiped away a reluctant tear that was slipping out of the corner of his eye. That tear said more than a torrent could have— about how the compassion of a woman and mother had, at least for the moment, broken through and soothed his weary and fearful soul.

A few years later, I traveled in Tanzania visiting AIDS-orphaned children with a woman from a very different background. Evelyn was Tanzanian, part of an organized group of volunteers that was caring for orphans and vulnerable children in their own community. Evelyn and I went to visit Rosie and her two sisters, who, like John and his brothers, made up a child-headed household. Theirs was again a miserable story, having lived parentless by themselves for over three years, and I sensed a deep loneliness. "We love it when Evelyn comes," they told me. "She's the only person who comes to visit." To say it was a difficult visit is a gross understatement; their faces have haunted me for years since.

Riding back in our vehicle, I asked Evelyn why she gave so much energy and time every week to being a volunteer helping orphans and vulnerable children. "No child should live like that!" she replied, with the indignation of just about any mother anywhere. "My children have their mother," she explained, while nearby there were children like Rosie who had neither mother nor father. Evelyn believed that it's part of her responsibility before God to care for those children too. It's very simple: no child should live without the watch care of a compassionate adult, not if Evelyn could do something about it. Her response was immediate and caring.

Women everywhere carry a great mantle of authority as nurturers and caregivers. Kay from suburban California and Evelyn from rural Tanzania both feel it. Both pushed past revulsion or shock better than most of us men, and they extended arms of love that reach across chasms of culture and spasms of pain to communicate, "Yes, you matter. You are one of us. You deserve motherly love and a compassionate touch. As long as we share this planet, you are important to me."

Our shared characteristics, which make us the same beneath our cultural differences, are truly the most beautiful aspects of what it means to be alive, to be human. And these similarities can forge bonds of connection that bridge over the gulches of cultures. These bonds of our common humanity can even withstand clashes between cultures—when we choose to let them.

> IN THE MOST IMPORTANT ASPECTS, WE ARE ALL THE SAME. AND THIS REALIZATION—THAT WE ARE ALL MEMBERS OF THE SAME HUMAN FAMILY—CAN CREATE BRIDGES OF CONNECTION AND COMPASSION THAT CAN SPAN ACROSS TOWN AND ACROSS THE WORLD.

THOSE WITH LITTLE TO GIVE TEACH ME MUCH ABOUT GENEROSITY

There are a great many lessons we can learn from those in poverty, but one lesson that humbles and stirs me over and over is the generosity of those with so little.

From Mother Teresa offering her own humble shawl to an elderly but wealthy American woman in a group I took to India, to meeting a homeless man near Los Angeles whose eulogy of a fellow street-dweller was that he always shared his precious "wake-up drink," to the tens of thousands of community volunteers in Africa who give from their own meager resources while caring for those dying of AIDS—praying with them, bathing them, washing their soiled bedding, and often using their own funds to buy them food and basic supplies—I am forever reminded of the generosity of the poor.

I'm also reminded that "from the one who has been entrusted with much, much more will be asked" (Luke 12:48), and this includes me.

If you think your income is nowhere near the top 1 percent, your worldview is too small. Just about everyone in America is in the top 2 percent of income levels globally, and most of us with full-time jobs are easily "one-percenters" on the global scale. (Find where you rank at GlobalRichList.com.)

I can't imagine standing in front of the other 99 percent and explaining why at times I, at the top of the global heap, feel financially stretched. But I won't have to stand in front of them, in this lifetime anyway, because I am not in close proximity with the global poor. And this skews my view of the truth of my material wealth.

An American colleague, Ashley, told of an indelible personal experience she'd had in the West African country of Niger. Living in a local village as a Peace Corps volunteer, Ashley ate daily with Madou, a wife and mother of three children. It was during a period of intense drought and declining food availability. One day Madou showed Ashley a bowl of millet and said somberly, "Ashley, this is all the food I have left in the house to feed my children."

Just then there was a knock on Madou's door. But instead of a savior bringing bags of food (don't you wish that's what happened?), there stood an old woman begging for food. As Ashley waited behind in the room, Madou reached into this same bowl and gave the beggar a generous scoop of grain. When Madou came back, Ashley asked her incredulously, "How could you do that when you have so little yourself?" Madou answered, "The beggar woman was a leper. It's true I have no food; but she has no hands."

I've never once been faced with such a riveting choice. But while Madou lives in close proximity to those in great need, I simply don't. I struggle often with that decision about location, and one day it may change. But for now, for me, I need to be very intentional about proactively reaching, mentally and emotionally, into places of need when I'm not there physically. I need to be continually mindful of the reality others face on a daily basis; I need to read, I need to watch, I need to care.

An American teenager I took with his father on a crosscultural trip came home and eventually convinced his family to sell their beach-community home and move to a more modest dwelling in order to have more funds available for being generous, and also to be in closer proximity to those in need. After high school this young man studied social services, and today he works in a helping profession.

A Mexican friend of mine grew up in a wealthy household in Mexico City. Then as a teen he lived for several months with an impoverished rural family as a volunteer. He was so moved by the generosity of those with so little that he later chose to spurn a lucrative career in the family business and instead work full-time to uplift the poor economically. He received his master's degree from the London School of Economics, and today, from his office in a disheveled neighborhood, he spends his time supporting microenterprises launched by the poor in his home country.

What you do personally about the lessons that you glean reflects your unique situation and spiritual journey. Each of us has a distinct temperament, calling, skill set, aptitude, and set of personal and family options. But Madou's example of sacrificial generosity is there for the taking, and it's hard to make a cross-cultural journey to a disadvantaged culture and not encounter similar examples. I've witnessed and experienced extravagant generosity from impoverished Muslims such as Madou and the Afari men in the previous chapter; from Christians of Roman Catholic, Protestant, and Orthodox backgrounds; from people of other religions and the nonreligious.

What is *generosity*, really? I have to stretch far beyond my own attempts to be generous to define it adequately and honestly. I think of those who have served people dying of AIDS, Ebola, or the plagues of old—who took mortal risks on behalf of others and sometimes died doing so. Giving despite one's own desperate need, like Madou did, is another example of putting one's very life in jeopardy in order to serve or save another. When I consider such self-sacrifice, I might define generosity this way: *Generosity can be measured as the added vulnerability we voluntarily expose ourselves to in order to reduce the vulnerability of others.* This is why Jesus, observing people put their offerings into the temple treasury, made this comment when a destitute widow dropped in two small coins: "Truly I tell you, this poor widow has put more into the treasury than all the others. They all gave out of their wealth; but she, out of her poverty, put in everything—all she had to live on" (Mark 12:43-44).

This understanding of generosity slithered up and bit me on a trip to Africa. Our group came across three excited boys, each about ten years old. One held out a stick with something dangling limp at the end of it, and I looked more closely and asked whether they had found a dead snake nearby. One of our local hosts matter-of-factly answered, "Oh, that's a cobra. They've just now killed it."

I was incredulous. After all, we'd just been walking through that area! What were young boys doing killing cobras?

"Oh, they *have to* kill it."

What?!

"Oh yes, if you see a poisonous snake, you must kill it. Otherwise, it may bite someone else."

Wait, what? That single statement opened up a window into an entire worldview. These boys did not kill the cobra in self-defense? Human nature would say, "Run away, very fast!" But in rural Africa, seeing a poisonous snake creates a social responsibility to the larger community that outweighs even one's personal safety.

Seeing that cobra suddenly required these young boys to put themselves into harm's way because of the possibility that someone else could be harmed and even killed by that snake at some unknown future time. They voluntarily exposed themselves to added vulnerability *in order to reduce the vulnerability of others*.

When generosity is viewed in this way, it becomes very clear that most of us in the world's wealthier countries know very little about being truly generous. In contrast to Madou or the boys with the cobra, we spend a great deal of our time, energy, and money to eliminate any sense of personal vulnerability whatsoever.

This reality check also challenges my perception of my needs versus my wants, of what I truly need versus what I choose to have. And I realize some newfound freedom: I can *choose* differently.

I might glibly say, paraphrasing 1 Chronicles 29:14, "Everything I have comes from you, Lord!" But the rest of that verse reads, "and we have given you only what comes from your hand." All I can do is give back, for God's use and glory, that which I've received from God's hand. *How much of what God puts into my hands is supposed to be mine to keep?*

THE GENEROSITY OF THE POOR SWEEPS AWAY OUR EXCUSES THAT WE CANNOT AFFORD TO ACT IN THE FACE OF HUMAN NEED. YET IT ALSO PROVIDES A MODEL FOR RESPONDING: BY SIMPLY SHARING WHAT GOD HAS PLACED IN OUR HANDS.

Madou, a humble Muslim woman, quite possibly illiterate, seems to understand this biblical principle better than I do. At least, she seems to more readily live it out. She doesn't just eat out of God's hand—from what little she's been given, with great vulnerability but greater obedience and trust in her Provider, she shares what's there and puts it into the hand of another.

⁂

The selected treasures in this chapter are certainly not intended to be exhaustive, and they are hardly unique to me. But they do help illustrate some of the powerful takeaways from our crosscultural experiences that can actually affect our ongoing lives, alter our choices and priorities, and deepen our future interactions across cultures.

For instance, when I encounter someone in a new setting, I'm now less likely to make a mental snap judgment, such as "This person is just *weird!*" Though I still falter, I'm more likely to see beyond the obvious differences and recognize our common humanity and build bridges of understanding from there.

Reading a Maya Angelou poem about our commonalities or hearing Ashley's story of Madou are wonderful springboards to reflecting on my own experiences and those of people I've met from other cultures. They help me unearth other treasures buried in my own lived experience, examine them more closely, gain fresh insights, and apply principles that can continue to teach and change me years later.

This is the great value of processing our experiences for a lifetime: as you keep digging into them, the veins of gold go deeper. And as a result, our lives become richer.

5

I think about Fedista. She has HIV. Her husband died of AIDS a few years ago, and now she's a single mother raising her daughter. Yet she's on a ministry team of people who help the sick. I keep her photo on my fridge. Behind her in the photo is her rented home—the size of a pool pump-house. Carved on a board over her front door are these words: "With Jesus All Things Are Possible." I've never in my life met anyone who more exuded the joy of the Lord than she did. Wow. When I think I have problems, I just stand quietly in my kitchen and look at Fedista's photo. She gives me perspective, and she gives me strength. — JANET

The surest way to continue having an impact after your crosscultural encounter is to intentionally foster ongoing connections—with the people and places you visited or with the issues that affect them. These connections will prompt you to pray, and as you go about your day you will find yourself more aware that life is also going on in that other place that now holds a part of your heart, with its challenges, hopes, joys, and struggles. Those didn't end when you came home, and your engagement with them shouldn't end either.

In fact, *one of the best predictors of true life change from your crosscultural experience is whether you develop and nurture ongoing connections.*

So ponder this for a moment: two years from now, how would you like to answer the question, *How did my crosscultural experience lead to tangible positive change, both for me and for the people and communities I met?*

These post-trip connections and engagements may take many forms and can allow us to benefit many people, both there and here.

CONNECT FOR CHANGE

I have felt like a part of my heart was left there, but it's hard to live in my own culture without comparing constantly. So it's easier to compartmentalize the memories. But then, I feel disappointed.   — ANN

There are many ways to foster ongoing connections with those we meet on our journey, connections that water the seeds of relationship that were planted during our trip. Email and social media can renew and deepen your interpersonal connections and may even lead you to undertake efforts on behalf of the individuals, communities, and issues you now care about deeply.

A disturbing social issue that one of my trip teams encountered in Uganda provided me a unique opportunity to make an impact months later. Every year I try to take some time off between Christmas and New Year's Day. But I'll admit that on the final evening of this vacation, staring at the unknown work year ahead is always a bit daunting. This time, however, I avoided the usual pity party. Instead, as I took a shower, I found myself reflecting on that Uganda trip nearly a year earlier.

Among visits to multiple programs, our team had an up-close look at the horrible practice of child ritual sacrifice that has arisen in the eastern provinces over the past ten to twenty years. Paid abductors slip into rural areas to snatch a child for their blood and body parts, which are used in ritualistic sacrifices for fertility or business success. Out of desperation and dark superstition, the "customers" find some tainted traditional healer in the area to hire the abductor-killer. It's an understatement to say this practice is terrorizing families in the region. World Vision has an excellent program to help these communities create and operate a creative rural AMBER Alert system, complete with drums, village megaphones, cellphone alerts, and the deputizing of motorcycle taxis to block the escapes. Within eighteen months, the program saw a stunning 88 percent reduction in abduction cases.

But I was remembering the distraught families we met when my group visited, and remembering with great frustration that the abductors were largely still on the loose, able to strike again. It was a chilling thought, and I knew this was causing deep, ongoing emotional trauma in this region, especially for the children.

Much has been done to mobilize the communities to rescue abducted children before it's too late, thanks to the heroic efforts of Bodai, the project leader, and the newly empowered citizenry. But Bodai, who never seems to lack a courageous smile, carries his own lunch with him every day—to avoid the possibility of being poisoned by those who consider his efforts a threat to their livelihood or their dark arts.

I thought about the insidious evil that powers this practice and how it needed to be finally rooted out. But there was clearly still a challenge with carrying out the arrest and prosecution of the perpetrators. Something needed to be done. This was the weak link in the chain of ending this terrible practice altogether!

I'd heard of an American lawyer and law professor who was voluntarily consulting with the legal system in Uganda, including its Supreme Court, so I jumped on the internet to find out more. I discovered we shared a mutual friend who could connect us. Through a few emails and voicemails, we made a connection between Bodai and this lawyer, and six months later they met in person in Uganda.

I later received the encouraging news that they were planning to jointly hold a conference for key Ugandan judges. The judges would be asked to commit to ending child sacrifice and expedite the legal process. They also intend to further engage other humanitarian groups in Uganda that address children's wellbeing.

How gratifying this was! The half-joking axiom that there are no more than six degrees of separation between you or me and anyone else on earth suddenly seemed more true as I discovered I was only three connections from the chief justice of the Ugandan Supreme Court!

It was humbling to personally play even a tiny role in addressing such a terrible scourge so far away, even beyond the funds my wife and I are contributing. How many times over the years have I dismissed seemingly crazy ideas like that, certain that I was powerless to make any impact? That prompting in the shower nudged me onto my computer, where I discovered a potential connection, and I made the effort over the following months to keep the connection alive until a meeting could take place. And now a new army of judges may soon be recruited into the battle against this menace.

One key to making our crosscultural experiences transformative is to have ongoing engagement with the issues we confronted and the people we met. Bodai risks his life daily, attacking this tragedy from every angle. I found one small yet tangible way I could strive with him in his tireless efforts, putting another tool in his hands. Continually emailing him for updates might be more of a burden than an encouragement to Bodai, distracting him from his critical work. But I can support him—in prayer, and sometimes in additional ways.

Missions and service organizations are sometimes cautious about encouraging direct connections between trip participants and their host communities because of the potential for unhappy outcomes, such as someone asking you for money for a need you can't verify. Cultural differences and language barriers, exacerbated by economic disparities, can lead to misunderstandings, abuse, and heartache. It's important to carefully avoid these pitfalls, yet wise connections, in tandem with good coaching from your trip leader, can minimize the risk.

You may not have yet found a meaningful way to stay engaged with a person or issue. Don't try to manufacture it. But do strain to keep your heart connected, be aware of what most stirred you, and be willing to walk through the doors that God opens. If you stay attentive, if you don't run from the difficult memories or fill your mind and calendar with distractions, you can trust God to show you appropriate next steps at the right time. If you've been home for some time now and haven't yet fostered points of reconnection, set aside time to pray about this and to examine whether you've left space in your heart and schedule to be able to pursue the promptings you receive. These ongoing connections are vital, but—just like anything you do with or for your friends—they require effort.

Have you fostered any ongoing connections with those you met or with the issues and challenges they and their culture may face? Do you wish you had done so? Does the idea of connecting with those you met bring up any fears? How could you connect in a way that addresses or mitigates these fears? How does the concept of six degrees of separation make you think differently about the unique impact you might make?

Fostering ongoing connections with people and issues you encountered also helps your brain make its own connections—perhaps between the water you drink and what people drink there, or how you buy your coffee and how much rural coffee growers earn, or the quality of education your children receive (or you've received) versus what is available for those you visited and now care about deeply.

You may be thinking: *I'm not sure that I want to have those thoughts! This is exactly what I don't want to feel. Who needs the guilt?*

But the truth is, this isn't guilt. It's recognizing our interconnectedness—that our different worlds exist side by side, in tandem.

Philosopher and activist Joanna Macy gives a provocative invitation:

Apathy and denial stem not from callous indifference or ignorance so much as fear of pain. . . . That [realization] became the most pivotal point in the landscape of my life . . . to see how we are called to not run from the discomfort or the

outrage or even fear. If we can be fearless, be with our pain, it
turns. It's not static. If we can . . . observe it in our hands and
keep breathing, it turns to reveal its other face: Our love for the
world, our absolute inseparable connectedness with all of life.

Can we have the courage to push through our own discomfort to
suddenly discover what's on the other side of it—perhaps our love
for the world? Can we be aware without despair? Awareness can
prompt prayer. Or ongoing financial support. Or action. By pushing
past the dark coats of discomfort and fear in our wardrobe, might
we find Aslan waiting for us?

During the final hours of my year-end holiday, instead of sulking
about the end of my vacation I let my heart be stirred once more,
opened my computer, and may have helped catalyze systemic change—change that could save the lives of precious children half a world away.

NURTURE A CONNECTION WITH SOMEONE YOU MET, OR TAKE ON AN ISSUE THAT MOVED YOU. THAT PERSON OR ISSUE IS YOUR PORTAL BACK INTO THAT CULTURE, AN ONGOING CONNECTION TO EVERYTHING THAT TOUCHED YOU ON YOUR JOURNEY, AND A MEANINGFUL WAY TO HOLD ON TO IT— PERHAPS FOR A LIFETIME.

How can your crosscultural experience help *you* make an impact on those you met or the issues they face?

FIND SOME CO-CONSPIRATORS

*Sitting in the Miami airport on the way home with all those teenagers, I knew my
life had to change.*
                                                                          — **ELIZABETH**

Just as a cord of three strands is not easily broken, your ongoing engagement will be strengthened when you can connect and collaborate with others who share your new awareness and passion. This might include team members from your crosscultural trip, others who have had similar experiences, or even a virtual group spread far apart. You're not alone in your passions and stirrings, nor in feeling powerless or overwhelmed. There is strength and energy in connecting with other like-minded people, and this is probably the best protection against the snare of apathy and inattention.

It's amazing what can be accomplished among friends who share a passion. That was certainly the experience of my friend Elizabeth. Nearly thirty years ago she made her first trip to a developing nation, visiting Haiti as an adult sponsor of a church youth trip. She recounts:

> I was so emotionally moved . . . the smells, the sounds . . . they didn't go away. Sitting in the Miami airport on the way home with all those teenagers, I knew my life had to change. I knew it within.
>
> I found some other women in my local area who had recently been to Guatemala with World Vision, so I went to meet them. They too had a desire to do something and we started a group together we called Women of Vision.
>
> We organized a crosscultural study group and began reading books about various issues around the world. The studies that pulled in Scriptures about God's concern for the poor really jumped off the page. Matthew 25 hit me the most:

that what we do for "the least of these" is what we do for Jesus. I probably smoothed over some of those hard verses at first, but as I've grown I'm more open to those truths.

I discovered Richard Foster's book *Freedom of Simplicity* and asked some friends to study the book with me, to discuss our lifestyles and how could we grow spiritually and learn to live on less so others could simply live.

Over time, we slowly began to saturate ourselves. Not everyone in the group or who went on trips "got it," which is my biggest disappointment. Some just wanted to take trips.

I get discouraged about poverty sometimes too, but I know there will be setbacks. I think it's my walk with Jesus and my spiritual grounding that keep me committed. You can't deny that God loves the poor and wants us all to be involved. It's God's work; we're just here to help. So, I don't succumb to discouragement.

LIFE CHANGE BY DEFINITION MEANS LASTING CHANGE. CONNECTING WITH FELLOW JOURNEYERS FROM YOUR TRIP TEAM, IN YOUR TOWN, THROUGH AN ESTABLISHED ORGANIZATION, OR IN AN ONLINE NETWORK CAN GREATLY MULTIPLY YOUR IMPACT AND GO A LONG WAY TOWARD BRINGING LASTING CHANGE, FOR YOURSELF AS WELL AS FOR THOSE PEOPLE AND ISSUES YOU NOW CARE ABOUT DEEPLY.

Over the years this group of women have learned together, stretched one another, and given each other courage they would not have had otherwise. In the process, they've fed the hungry in the inner city, supported women coming out of prison, organized dozens of crosscultural exposure trips locally and around the world, contributed more than $7 million for global poverty programs on four continents, and facilitated over 2,500 children being supported through child sponsorship. They've also inspired other women around the country to start similar groups in their own areas.

As the African proverb says, "If you want to go *fast*, go alone. But if you want to go *far*, go with others."

THE TRIP'S *NOT* THE THING

To me, a life-changing experience is one that causes an internal transformation. . . .
A force inside compels us to begin a journey of discovery—causing us to ponder
the nature and nurture of the gifts we have been given to promote change.

— JENNIFER

Much of the time, our expectations of crosscultural trips are backwards. We think the journey is about the service we perform *during* the trip. In other words, we think that the trip's the thing—that we went because we were needed while we were there.

It is true: we *are* needed! But not in the way you might be thinking.

My wife, Janet, and I were moved by meeting Angela in Gulu, Uganda. Angela had been kidnapped from her school at age fourteen and forced to "marry" a commander of the infamous guerilla group the Lord's Resistance Army (LRA). Angela eventually bore two children by this LRA commander. Finally, in 2004, after eight terrible years of captivity in the bush, she was able to escape with her children. Afterward she went through a painful recovery process at the World Vision Children of War Center. But more than a decade later this region is still traumatized from the LRA's twenty-year campaign of terror. Even the child brides and child soldiers the LRA conscripted under threat of death are often spurned by their communities, who deem them complicit in the violence that wracked this region. Worse yet, the offspring of these forced brides are ostracized because they were fathered by LRA soldiers. To address this issue, Angela and another escapee-mother launched an outreach program named Wayte Ki Gen (We Have Hope). WKG assists mothers and children who are essentially homeless because of the stigma they still suffer and who struggle to earn a living.

Several months after our return from Uganda, I was contacted by a foundation director who would soon be making her own trip there. She asked me for ways to learn more about the LRA's destructive legacy. Since she was traveling to Gulu, I described Angela's compelling story, commended WKG, and then connected them directly.

After a very brief but positive meeting during that trip, the director asked a trusted organization to assess WKG and assist them in creating a multiyear strategic plan. Eventually I received a note of gratitude from the foundation and learned that they had made a significant grant to launch WKG's work in earnest. Angela was exhilarated, the foundation was delighted, and my wife and I were thrilled. And it began simply because I had the opportunity to be a voice for WKG once I was back home.

Let's face it: unless you're a professional using your expertise (such as a volunteer doctor or dentist), any work you may have performed on your crosscultural journey could probably have been done more expertly by someone else. But no one is as effective as you in being a voice within your own sphere of influence for the people and issues to which you were exposed. *Whatever service you may have provided during your trip is tiny compared to the service you can provide after you return.*

There are many ways you can proactively use your voice—an informal chat with a friend from your church, work, or social network; a meeting with a kindred spirit to encourage their involvement or conspire on how to make a deeper impact together; small group presentations or even fundraising events.

Often these opportunities are so natural that we don't even realize we are speaking up for those without another voice in these circles. At other times speaking up is a conscious decision—perhaps not something we crave personally but that we do anyway out of solidarity with those in need and obedience to God's prompting.

Don't fall into the trap of thinking, *But I'm not qualified!* You are imminently qualified to share your personal experience!

When you do have the chance to use your voice, remember to not make it about you. It's important that you highlight the resources and resourcefulness that already existed within the community and that you personally encountered—such as the people's resilience, industriousness, creativity, volunteer spirit, generosity, or ability simply to survive despite immense obstacles—hopefully illustrated through your unique picture-window story. Don't fixate solely on needs you saw or on what small service you and your team may have performed there. These are people with dignity and humanity, and they have amazing capabilities and personal assets, not only deficits and challenges. *Speak of them as you would want*

to be spoken about were you in their shoes, and as they deserve to be
spoken about.

There are times when these opportunities to be a voice come to
us quite unexpectedly, such as when we are contacted by an up-
coming traveler as I was, or when someone you know asks for a
recommendation on a trustworthy charitable cause to support. But
even the unexpected opportunities require your proactive choices:
a willingness to speak up, to risk showing more enthusiasm than
your friend might prefer, to keep your heart connected with people
and cultures you now know and love and with whom you have the
opportunity to partner and strive—together.

Keep in mind also that everyone recognizes the importance of due
diligence—checking out issues or organizations or movements they
have an interest in before getting
involved. But many don't have
the time to do this important
work themselves, so instead
they simply don't get involved.
However, if someone they know
and respect has already checked
it out (in your circle of trust,
that's *you*), then they are much
more likely to jump in if you
show them the way. You are providing a valuable service to them,
and in turn they may join you in
a cause that is dear to you.

**YOUR TRIP WAS NOT THE
THING; IT'S THE SPRING.
IT'S NOT THE END OF YOUR
SERVICE BUT ONLY THE
BEGINNING OF YOUR REAL
EFFECTIVENESS. YOU MAY NOT
HAVE KNOWN THE LANGUAGE
OF THOSE YOU VISITED
DURING YOUR TRIP, BUT YOU
DO KNOW THE LANGUAGE
BACK HOME. AND THIS IS FAR
MORE IMPORTANT BECAUSE
YOU ARE NOW EQUIPPED TO
RENDER A SERVICE THAT YOU
ARE UNIQUELY QUALIFIED FOR:
BEING AN EFFECTIVE VOICE
FOR THE VOICELESS WITHIN
YOUR SPHERE OF INFLUENCE.**

Out of your desire to serve those you met on your crosscultural journey, what are some ways you might proactively be a voice for them in your sphere of influence? Are there local opportunities for advocacy or action on an issue that touched you? How might you expand and deepen your learning in order to become a more effective advocate?

YOUR STORIES CAN CHANGE THE WORLD

My friend and colleague Kari Costanza tells an inspiring example of how a traveler's experience can change the world, or at least a corner of it—especially when they focus on a particular person.

The best stories are about people, because people connect with other people more than they do with programs. But in connecting with people, they learn what a program does and why it is so valuable.

That happened in Ethiopia with Mark. Mark went to Ethiopia with his wife, Jennifer, in January 2013. To understand the need for water, Mark and Jennifer visited a dirty stream, the only source near this community for fetching water. He could see the dirt in the water and how the animals drank from the same stream that people bathed and drank from. They met a father named Kuma at the stream, and Mark asked to carry one of the five-gallon containers full of water back to Kuma's house.

It was a difficult task for Mark, trudging up that long hill. All along the way, a woman named Berket walked alongside Mark, offering to help him with his burden. By the time he got to Kuma's house, Mark was exhausted. Berket asked him if he'd like some milk to drink to make his muscles grow.

Kuma invited Mark and Jennifer inside his humble home and told them the story of his family—how lack of water was straining his marriage; how he was suffering from trachoma; and worst of all—how the couple had lost Chaltu, their happy little sprite of a daughter, to water-borne disease.

Mark drank it all in.

Then he returned to Texas and told this story to others—mostly people who knew and respected Mark—using photos of those interactions and of his water-carrying journey as a guide. Mark so inspired his friends that they were able to contribute $375,000 to fully underwrite a pipeline which would soon supply Kuma's family and his entire community of 7,500 people with clean water!

It all happened because Mark shared his story. Stories can change the world.

Mark connected with real people, he learned about the underlying issues they face, and he returned home determined and equipped to be a credible and passionate voice within his sphere of influence—simply using his personal story from the trip. As a result, a huge number of people in that community Mark cares about will never be the same. For Mark and Jennifer, it doesn't get much better than that.

There's another important aspect to this story: Mark and Jennifer didn't sell their home and business to go drill wells in Ethiopia themselves. They didn't change *what* they do; they changed *why* they do it.

Donald Miller, in the preface to his book *A Million Miles in a Thousand Years: How I Learned to Live a Better Story*, makes a powerful case for having the right *why* in life:

> If you watched a movie about a guy who wanted a Volvo and worked for years to get it, you wouldn't cry at the end when he drove off the lot, testing the windshield wipers. You wouldn't tell your friends you saw a beautiful movie or go home and put a record on to think about the story you'd seen. The truth is, you wouldn't remember that movie a week later, except you'd feel robbed and want your money back. Nobody cries at the end of a movie about a guy who wants a Volvo.
>
> But we spend our lives actually living those stories, and expect our lives to feel meaningful. The truth is, if what we choose to do with our lives won't make a story meaningful, it won't make a life meaningful either.

Mark and Jennifer know what they are good at, and they see their business, their relationships, and their credibility all as tools for God's kingdom use and for caring about others. They know they're not experts in drilling wells; you probably aren't either. But here's the good news: whatever we have, our whole LIFE—labor, influence, finances, and experience—can be an offering that God will use, if we are willing.

And in the process we too can live a story worth making a life out of.

6

I did not know what to expect, except that I would probably get dysentery. I was not seeking a drastic change in direction . . . my transformation was unexpected and a priceless gift.   — CAROL

You may feel it's too soon to begin considering *another* crosscultural trip, but remember: you don't have to board an airplane to encounter other cultures! And now that you've had at least one meaningful experience, you will discover new opportunities all around you to pay attention to and connect with people from different backgrounds and customs from your own.

At the same time, if you returned from your trip with nagging concerns about the actual value of what you did, if you worry about whether you have truly empowered people or have instead fostered dependency, or if you're feeling disappointed with how little time was devoted to delving into the underlying problems behind the situations you saw and the people you met, then you'll be glad to know that although no experience is perfect, some trips are definitely better than others. More importantly, there are concrete ways to make your *next* trip your best trip yet.

The desire to open ourselves to another culture and to serve the other is a beautiful thing, often a spiritual milestone and one of our most selfless decisions. But making the best use of that good intention—for the travelers as well as for those who receive and host them—is a major challenge.

Let's look at some of the most common shortcomings of these trips and what can be done to improve them. As you do, keep in mind that as a consumer of crosscultural experiences, *your* expectations are critical—they can either perpetuate the status quo or help bring about systemic improvements for everyone involved.

EMPOWERING OTHERS BEATS "ACCOMPLISHING" SOMETHING YOURSELF

I've seen and experienced myself the strong desire of teens and young adults (even mature adults) to try to give the poor . . . more Western comforts—to alleviate the short-termer's guilt about his/her relative comfort versus those he/she is attempting to serve. This false compassion often leads to creating dependency rather than pursuit of self-development.   — **ROBERT**, DENOMINATIONAL LEADER

Numerous times, I've seen the destructive aftereffects of well-meaning groups who arrive for a week or a month, have their serving experience, take their photos, and leave. But poverty, marginalization, violence, hopelessness, and similar challenges are long-term problems requiring long-term solutions. Recent important books such as *When Helping Hurts*, *Helping Without Hurting in Short-Term Missions*, and *Toxic Charity* point out the many careful considerations required, as well as unseen traps in effectively helping others without creating or perpetuating dependency. (Any parent will testify what a challenge this can be!) Well-meaning groups with little understanding of this dynamic can disrupt and derail community-organized initiatives, as well as hamper the efforts of serious development practitioners attempting to empower local communities in raising up their *own* solutions to their challenges. Such trips break the first rule of effective service: *do no harm.*

A few years ago, I volunteered with a church team from southern California for a day trip to Tijuana, Mexico, where we were to build a very simple house in one day. The concrete pad was already in place, the materials were ready for us, and our focus was to construct the small but sturdy building. I can't call it a *home*, because I believe the family intended to have only a couple of their children sleep there—their larger existing home was adjacent to the new structure. The family members helped in the construction, it's true; I hammered nails into the shingles with the matriarch. But why wouldn't they help? This was a fantastic opportunity for them to acquire a significant new asset at no cost beyond patience and a little labor.

The key goal of our group was not to learn, nor to get to know the family. We had far too large a horde of volunteers for meaningful conversation, though I tried to converse with the mother, albeit without translation. The American-led nonprofit that hosted us was tasked with prescreening the recipients, preparing the site for us, and providing a foreman—not a translator. We were there simply as untrained construction laborers. Little effort was made to facilitate any personal connections and no effort at all to help us understand the underlying issues of poverty, housing, land ownership challenges, rural-to-urban migration, and so on.

Apparently, it was decided long before we arrived that cluttering our minds with these complex problems might distress our happy crew and discourage people from returning to volunteer the next year. Instead, our goal was kept very simple: to have a sense of accomplishment, leave behind a structure, take some photos, pray for the family, and report it all triumphantly back home at church the following Sunday.

Such experiences have been critiqued as "guilt offsetting" trips, designed to mitigate the negative impact of our consumerist lifestyles the other 364 days of the year. It's also easy for us to feed our own egos through our service, and in the process disempower those we wanted to help.

Here's the challenge: when trip leaders organize crosscultural experiences, they have to consider not only the needs of those who will be served, but *even more so* the expectations of those participating or those they hope might participate. To the degree that our expectations as participants are focused on some sense of personal accomplishment or sacrifice or whatever else *we* expect to gain from the experience, the focus of the trip will be skewed further away from maximizing the benefit to those we came to serve toward maximizing the sense of gratification we receive. Why?

THE MORE WE REQUIRE A SENSE OF PERSONAL ACCOMPLISHMENT OR FOCUS ON WHAT WE'LL GET OUT OF THE EXPERIENCE, THE HIGHER THE LIKELIHOOD WE WILL DO LITTLE IF ANYTHING USEFUL AND POSSIBLY EVEN DAMAGE ANY POSSIBILITY FOR TRUE PROGRESS AMONG THOSE WE SEEK TO SERVE.

Because in order to successfully attract a team, the trip leader must factor our personal expectations into the trip's design to some degree.

Better trips start with better expectations. And that change starts with us.

WE SERVE BEST BY LEARNING FIRST

How can I help [travelers] take what they've learned and begin to live a servant lifestyle, not just on the [missions trip], but throughout their lives? I don't have the answer. — LAURIE, CHURCH MISSIONS TRIP LEADER

In university and college settings, crosscultural trips are often set up as "service learning" opportunities. The idea is to learn *by* serving. Sounds reasonable at first blush. But two veteran organizers of service learning trips had an epiphany of how backward this idea truly is, because it assumes we can serve effectively without learning first!

These leaders, Claire Bennett and Daniela Papi, have created an organization called Learning Service that turns the common concept on its head. As they contend in the *Stanford Social Innovation Review*, our crosscultural encounters should first and foremost be learning experiences, during which we get to know the people and the context of those we hope to serve; then we serve them *once we are home*. By focusing the crosscultural experience on interpersonal relationship—true crosscultural encounters—and wrestling with the social, religious, and economic issues confronting that community and their culture, we can return home as aware, articulate advocates. By deepening our understanding and heightening our passions through the trip, we are equipped to organize, educate, donate, raise up resources and energy from within our sphere of influence, and much more. The sky is the limit when we realize that our most important *doing* begins when we get back home.

Rich Stearns, president of World Vision and bestselling author of *The Hole in Our Gospel*, points out that effectively alleviating poverty is like rocket science. I'd say it's even more difficult. Not to downplay the tireless efforts and brilliance of rocket scientists, but issues of disparity, marginalization, and systemic injustice have proved to be far more difficult to solve than getting a person into space. While the percentage of the global population living in extreme poverty is at its lowest in human history and dropping steadily, there are still grave, intractable issues to solve. And the world needs all hands on deck to solve them.

If I had a teenage son who wanted to be a brain surgeon, I would never suggest he start by simply performing some brain surgeries! No, he would first have to endure many years of schooling, many months of practicums, and a great deal of mentoring. Yet with our world's most challenging and enduring human problems, we oversimplify the solutions in order to hand them to minimally trained volunteers from another culture who often don't speak the language, and then we expect them to do something useful and not harmful in a day, a week, or even a few months.

Instead, just think of this: because of the incredible opportunities for travel that are available today, we can become educated, aware, and engaged global citizens, not serving several days once in our lifetime or even once a year, but serving *every day* by how we live, what we read and discuss, how we vote, and how we use our time, voice, and resources on behalf of others. It is this work that should not be left to the professionals! Every one of us must be involved in this effort.

Why be involved? Because this engagement mirrors the vision Jesus shared with his followers over and over. He called it the kingdom of heaven or the reign of God, and he calls us to follow him in working toward it. Remember the kingdom? We pray for it every time we recite the Lord's Prayer: "Thy kingdom come, thy will be done *on earth*, as it is in heaven." The kingdom is the place where the poor are blessed, those who mourn are comforted, the blind are given sight, those who were naked are clothed and warm.

Jesus announced his entire ministry by reading the words of Isaiah 61 in public:

> "The Spirit of the Lord is on me,
>
>> because he has anointed me
>>
>> to proclaim good news to the poor.
>
> He has sent me to proclaim freedom for the prisoners
>
>> and recovery of sight for the blind,
>
> to set the oppressed free,
>
>> to proclaim the year of the Lord's favor."

The dramatic scene ends with these words:

> Then he rolled up the scroll, gave it back to the attendant and sat down. The eyes of everyone in the synagogue were fastened on him. He began by saying to them, "Today this scripture is fulfilled in your hearing." (Luke 4:18-21)

We, as his disciples, those who seek to follow in Jesus' footprints, are to be doing this same life-giving, life-restoring work—not once, not once a year, but every day. When we do so, we also fulfill this Scripture in the spirit of Jesus.

And there's more. Our world needs us, needs us to break through beyond our own cultural myopia to be effective global citizens. We are the most resourced, most collectively powerful generation that has ever lived in the entire history of the world. And our global neighbors need us to understand and to be involved—not as experience-hungry *voluntourists* but as engaged *neighbors*, working to build crosscultural understanding, effect social change, and express the compassion of Jesus in ways that truly help others.

The expression "think globally; act locally" has never made more sense: use your next trip to learn and think about the issues, then return as a global citizen to act and advocate in your own locale on behalf of those very issues and people.

ON YOUR NEXT TRIP, FOCUS ON LEARNING AND CONNECTING. ENGAGE THE ISSUES, TAKE NOTES LIKE A STUDENT, AND THEN BECOME A CHANGE AGENT BACK HOME FOR GOD'S KINGDOM TO COME MORE FULLY ON EARTH—FOR THE SAKE OF THOSE YOU MET AND THE MILLIONS MORE THEY REPRESENT.

THE MINISTRY OF PRESENCE

Let this darkness be a bell tower and you the bell. As you ring, what batters you becomes your strength.

— RAINER MARIE RILKE, "LET THIS DARKNESS BE A BELL TOWER"

Perhaps the most meaningful service we can provide during our crosscultural experience is the ministry of presence. Simply being *with* another, giving them attention, and taking time to learn their story, encourage their often heroic efforts in the face of enormous odds, and understand the challenges they face can have tremendously positive impact.

Let's face it: most of a person's greatest struggles in life are long-term challenges, and those can't possibly be fixed by us on a short-term visit. But when we spend time listening to someone's story and asking thoughtful questions to increase our understanding, inviting them to give voice to their fears, joys, and hopes, both parties are blessed.

We all know what a gift it is when we feel truly heard by another person. We feel valued and cared for, our burden seems somehow shared and even lightened, and we are *en*couraged—infused with added courage to carry on and prevail over our challenges. This is the gift we give to others when we are truly *present* with them.

By being present in this way, we become far more aware of the underlying challenges and issues and better understand how they affect the lives of real people—people with names and stories that we now know. And as a result, we are better able to consider how to make a truly meaningful long-term difference toward these issues once we return home.

For me, the ministry of presence is a primary focus for every crosscultural encounter. In fact, my choice of the word *encounter* throughout this book presupposes such active engagement with people. In this ministry we are not swinging a hammer, but we are working nonetheless: working hard to show up mentally and relationally, to stay engaged even when we are very tired and emotionally overloaded, and to lean in to each person's story, even the painful stories.

On one trip to the Afar region of Ethiopia, our travel team met with a support group for people living with HIV and AIDS. Our group didn't understand who we would be meeting that morning until we arrived, and it took us all aback for a moment. But once we got our bearings, one of us, then another, and soon all of us stepped forward to shake hands with the people seated in the front row. We very intentionally pushed our chairs forward so we could be close to them while we listened to their stories. In doing so, many on the team were pushing past personal fears, and for them these forms of being present were a real act of service to our hosts.

After listening to some initial comments from the support group members, we asked them how their families had responded upon learning their loved one was HIV-positive. That's when the crowded room became a holy sanctuary. One by one, reluctantly at first, they feebly stood and spoke:

"My family won't touch me anymore. They won't let me eat from the same dish. I'm an outcast."

"I had to leave home and rent a room in another house. After a while the family there wouldn't let me use the toilet. They finally made me sleep outside."

A woman stood and bemoaned through her tears, "Last night I was forced out of my own house. What will I do now?"

Many in the room poured out heart-rending stories of their struggles. It was utterly overwhelming. As their wretched reality sunk in, Stew, one of our team members began to cry silently. Some women in the support group noticed his tears, and they too began to weep. A holy connection was made as he shared their pain.

At one point our organizer told us that we needed to leave in order to maintain our schedule. But it was clear that there was no more important thing we could do in that moment than to simply stay and let these people pour out their hearts—outcasts who were so grateful to have someone else carry a small portion of their suffering.

So we altered our schedule.

Two years later, I took another group of visitors to Afar, and we spent time with this same support group. Initially this second team was even more hesitant to touch those with the HIV virus and generally stayed clumped together on one side of the room.

But after stories were shared, compassion replaced the initial caution. We all intermingled in a circle for a time of prayer where nearly everyone held their neighbor's hand. Then suddenly two things seemed to break—our group's fear and their group's sense of stigma and shame. Everyone roamed the room, hungry to touch and be touched. The HIV support group members eagerly clasped our hands in theirs, often leaning into us with a gentle shoulder bump that signifies added affection. Bringing down these walls with a caring touch of acceptance was our team's finest and truest act of service that day.

That evening, as our team debriefed with only a few flashlights by which to see each other, it was difficult to talk of anything but our morning's first stop: the encounter with the support group. After everyone else had shared, I shined a light toward Jen, who was silently sitting in shadow. When I asked if she had any thoughts, Jen quietly shared the rest—and the best—of the story.

As we said our goodbyes to the group, Jen felt moved to hug each woman as they left. So she staked out a strategic spot near the exit. One by one these women acquiesced to her gesture, until the last woman came up. Jen recalled, "At first she only wanted to shake my hand, even though she'd seen me hug others. But I pulled her close. Her initial stiffness melted away and then she squeezed me back tightly, pressing her head on my shoulder. Then she arched up and I felt her lips softly kiss my neck."

Leaping over all the language barriers and all the stigma, the kiss communicated everything.

After Jen's story, there was nothing left to say. We were all glad now to be in shadow, each lost in our own thoughts and prayers. Jen's response of unguarded compassion had melted a hungry heart. And when she shared her story, our hungry hearts were melted too.

Dr. Stan Mooneyham wrote,

In healing, whether bodies or minds, one cannot do anything significant without a "hands-on" attitude. While there's a certain professional detachment that enables a doctor or a pastor or social worker to deal with suffering, it is tragic for both parties when the doctor cannot hurt, the pastor cannot weep or the social worker cannot feel. It is the hurting, the weeping, the feeling that does at least part of the healing. Perhaps the larger part.

Jesus, the incarnation of God, came to be present with us. This *being with* was the most powerful aspect of his life's ministry. If we wish to follow Jesus, we too must be incarnational; we too must be present with people.

We seldom appreciate the influence we can have simply by *being with* someone as visitors from another country or community. Our presence can imbue with value those who lack self-worth, encourage

ON YOUR NEXT TRIP, MAKE IT A HIGH PRIORITY TO PRACTICE THE MINISTRY OF PRESENCE. AND IF YOUR SCHEDULE DOESN'T ALLOW IT, CHANGE YOUR SCHEDULE. those working hard to make a better life and world, bring attention to an issue, and help us better know what effective actions we might take back home on their behalf.

BALANCING ACTION AND REFLECTION

I absolutely brought back what I had hoped for: experiencing a rich, deep connection with others in another culture, insights into life in extreme poverty, and a compelling desire to discover . . . what do I do with this, and how do I gracefully allow myself to reintegrate into my old life? — JENNIFER

Just as Jen's story of an unexpected kiss stirred the rest of our group, a great deal of the learning on crosscultural trips happens because of intentional group reflection and debriefing at the end of each day.

Our culture has become accustomed to stringing one experience to another, with little to no space given for reflecting on the meaning of each one. Our society is partly responsible for this, but so is each of us. Habits of reflection and contemplation are personal behaviors, first and foremost.

Taking time with your tripmates to unpack each day at its end is a tremendous way to mine the treasure of your experiences. This doesn't need to be intense or formal; most often my groups do this over a relaxed dinner, hopefully after some rest and refreshment. I make it a practice to wash up and change clothes before we sit down for dinner, decompressing as I go through the motions and thereby preparing myself to listen to others in the group.

Recently I attended a reunion for a group of twenty-three people who had traveled together to Tanzania a few months earlier. Included in the team were a group of fourteen- and fifteen-year-olds. After we enjoyed reconnecting over a meal, we all circled around for what became two and a half hours of checking in with each other, hearing about each person's journey of returning home, and integrating our trip experiences into our lives. These were very normal American teens, yet not one of them squirmed or complained or checked out—because during our trip, our group's evening debriefs had added insight to each person's journey and communicated that each person's thoughts and feelings mattered. By the time we reunited, we all cared about each other, and no one wanted to miss another person's insight from which they too might learn.

Every person on a trip has a unique set of eyes and ears, not to mention sensitivities. Each one hears and sees and feels things that I miss—daily! Imagine how much more you could absorb if you had five or ten sets of eyes, ears, legs, hands, tears. Every person around the debrief circle learns much that they'd personally missed along the way.

On my trip to Afar, none of us knew Jen's story until she shared it that evening. Two years earlier, no one on our team knew Stew's story until our debrief: shortly after he cried with the HIV/AIDS group, Stew's nose began to bleed, and a local man helped clean him up and calm his emotions, even though Stew's crisis came during a pandemic of deadly blood-borne disease. The painful disparity between how the HIV/AIDS group members were treated by their fearful families and neighbors and how Stew had been treated tenderized our hearts that evening when he shared his story.

As the experiences on a trip pile up, we can begin to synthesize not only, *What did I see today?* but also, *What does it mean?* and even more deeply, *Why does this matter,* and *What does it mean for me to actually care about it?* Psychologists point out that these deeper questions are the ones that truly have the potential to transform us. Thus, debriefing our experiences at the end of each day helps these one-time encounters authentically lead to lifelong compassion, awareness, and even action. Make the effort to participate in these reflection discussions, and take responsibility for arranging informal dialogues if they are not planned.

Similarly, a debrief time at the end of a trip to wrap up the broad sweep of the experience and its meaning becomes both the dessert of the trip and the appetizer to life back home. Don't rush away without making time for this final gathering. This is where you begin to consider what you will pack in the suitcase of your mind, heart, and feet when you leave for home—far more important decisions than what clothes and trinkets you will carry back.

In addition to group discussions, or when there is no group, journaling the key aspects of your day either in the evening or the next morning is a personal practice that pays dividends far beyond the minor hassle it can seem to be. For some, blogging or sketching may be more meaningful outlets. But find something that allows you to be real with yourself and explore the deeper transformative questions, not simply a public chronicle of what you ate and where you slept, which far too many trip blogs tend to dwell on.

The point here is not to heap guilt on yourself to wring every possible lesson from each day in order not to miss a single thing God might have for you. But finding those personal habits that help you decompress and thoughtfully reflect—instead of rushing on to the next thing or checking out mindlessly—will allow you to sift through the many minor encounters and grasp the vital lessons worth bringing home and carrying in your pocket for a lifetime.

ACTION MUST BE BALANCED WITH REFLECTION FOR IT TO HAVE MEANING. DON'T NEGLECT THE NEED TO REFLECT DAILY ALONG YOUR JOURNEY, ON YOUR OWN AND WITH OTHERS. MAKE CERTAIN YOUR LEADER UNDERSTANDS THE VALUE YOU PLACE ON THIS TYPE OF REFLECTION, EACH DAY AND AT THE END OF THE TRIP. IF IT DOESN'T WORK WITH THE WHOLE GROUP, FIND A FEW THOUGHTFUL TEAM MEMBERS AND DEBRIEF WITH THEM.

If Socrates was correct that "the unexamined life is not worth living," then surely the unexamined crosscultural trip is not worth taking.

EMBRACING BOTH COMPASSION AND JUSTICE

This [trip] has spurred me to want to act on behalf of all those who are presently "the lost and the least." The "least" of course being all those marginalized, the ragged masses of those suffering the injustice of dehumanizing poverty as well as the world's scorn. The "lost" I frankly consider to be those of us in bondage to self-centered affluence. — RANDY

A decade ago, the term *justice*—as in "creating a more *just* world"— would make me recoil. It seemed like a mean-spirited finger wagged by so-called bleeding hearts to cause the rest of us to constantly feel bad. I'm certain that, deep down, I was afraid of feeling guilt.

It took me a long time to let the concept of justice stand on its own merits, without fleeing from it because of the unknown demands I feared it might place on me. The problem, in part, was that I suddenly started noticing it in the Bible and had to admit how little attention I'd given to what was actually being communicated there. What was God's passion for justice all about?

Let's be honest: *mercy* doesn't require that much of us. Mercy was historically the stuff of kings and others who dispensed power. Not only did it not require them to give up their power, but bestowing mercy often reinforced and accentuated their authority status. They could casually grant royal favor on their subjects, sparing their lives with magnanimous flair, and thereby curry loyalty along the populace. (Think of Pilate releasing Barabbas to the crowd.)

But in America and much of the world, our forebears saw the traditional system as inherently unjust, driven by capricious personality rather than representative democracy. I have been the beneficiary of those willing to fight for the ideal of consistent justice over inter-mittent, humanly rationed mercy.

The many examples in human history of justice seeking became touchstones for me. By recognizing how much *I* have benefitted from the struggles that others have fought for justice, I feel com-pelled to also fight for justice for the *other*. Working for justice for the benefit of others is, I believe, a higher calling than being mer-ciful, even when (maybe especially when) it requires sacrifice from me.

I volunteered for a year with Lights On, a program that assists the inmates who are released from our county jail nightly between 10:00 p.m. and 3:00 a.m. Like most jails, ours is not situated in the safest area, yet each weeknight twenty-five to seventy-five people were released onto the streets, women as well as men. The Lights On organizers saw this as a tragedy waiting to happen.

Each night Lights On parks its shabby but well-lit camper near the jail and places folding tables and chairs on the sidewalk. Re-leasees can borrow a phone, get some coffee and snacks, have a safe place to wait for a ride, or get directions to a bus.

For me, these nights became another powerful opportunity to practice the ministry of presence. I had deep conversations with some who had gotten messed up with drugs or the wrong crowd and who had a strong desire (at least in that moment) to never make the same mistake again. I would offer to pray for some, en-courage others in their journey, or simply help someone think about who they might call for a ride home. Most would call Mom.

Every night was a series of crosscultural encounters. And it didn't matter how hardened or gruff or mentally unstable a releasee appeared; they were incredibly grateful for our simple presence and humble offerings. They would help us set up our tables, clean up if they spilled coffee, or even make a donation out of gratitude.

I loved Lights On and I loved volunteering. I learned to love many of the people I met. And I think it's that final love—love for the releasees—that made me decide to try to kill the Lights On program.

Why? Because I came to believe it was unjust to release people from jail in the middle of the night. I believed the county needed to end nighttime releases, which of course would end the need for a safe and friendly nighttime outreach program. Yes, we had a captive, grateful clientele; it was a made-to-order outreach opportunity to a challenging population! I felt I was doing something useful and good. But the demand for our services was being created in part by a system that put releasees at unnecessary risk. How could I simply feed my own ego or justify a "witnessing opportunity" and ignore that injustice?

I decided to invite a judge I know to come volunteer one night; then he invited another judge. We connected with the longtime leader of an inner-city nonprofit nearby and with a young attorney. Together we created a little work team to explore the issues, from inside and outside the system.

A few months later, we were able to meet with most of our county's top law enforcement officials. Since then the number of people being released each night has been cut in half. I certainly can't claim that this reduction is directly related to our efforts, but we've seen tangible progress since we raised our voices.

Our efforts could eventually help shut down a program I loved and will miss. And please understand, I believe there is a real opportunity to benefit people's lives through Lights On.

But I realized that Lights On is a mercy ministry. And as critical as mercy ministries are, seeking to correct an underlying injustice is more important. *There are times when my commitment to justice must take precedence over the satisfaction of ministering to the victims of injustice.*

That choice isn't often required of me, but sometimes this is only because I don't make the effort to look any deeper. When we muster up the nerve to probe and ponder more deeply into root causes, and if we discover this is in fact the choice before us, may we have the courage to take the just road, not simply the merciful one.

Micah 6:8 makes clear the need to embrace *both* justice and mercy:

> And what does the LORD require of you?
> To act justly and to love mercy
>   and to walk humbly with your God.

I love extending mercy to others. Yet my Lord requires that I, with humility, seek justice for them as well.

Here's the challenge: the great majority of crosscultural outreach programs focus on acts of mercy, not on addressing long-term injustice or similar systemic issues. That's understandable; exercising our mercy muscle can give us the strength and courage to probe underlying justice issues.

For instance, much has been written recently about orphanage homes actually becoming a "growth industry" in some nations, while the majority of child residents still have one or both parents living. This expansion of orphanages is often due to volunteers from wealthier countries wanting an "orphan experience," then returning home to send money to support a few more children, effectively increasing the demand for more orphans. Talk about tragic unintended consequences!

Yet other orphanage volunteers come home disturbed; they loved interacting with the precious children, but they recognize that institutionalizing children is not the best solution. So they begin to look into the underlying issues of poverty, parenting, and Western paternalism that drive the industry and cause a child to be separated from their parents or extended family support system. These travelers become advocates for better solutions, such as those every developed country has long implemented, *even if this means* the eventual closure of the orphanages that gave them the emotional high and photo ops on prior trips.

ON YOUR NEXT TRIP, YOU CAN BE AN AGENT OF LONG-TERM CHANGE IF YOU MAKE THE EFFORT TO PROBE AND UNDERSTAND THE UNDERLYING ISSUES, HUMBLY SEEKING JUSTICE AS WELL AS LOVING MERCY.

In effect, this latter category of travelers became learners and then advocates for better solutions. And they will have the deep satisfaction of being systemic change agents for improved care of children caught in the web of poverty.

PONDERING AND PLANNING YOUR NEXT CROSSCULTURAL ENCOUNTER

Whatever purpose you thought you had for your prior crosscultural encounters, consider them learning experiences that you can continuously improve on. You can put the principles in this chapter into practice down the street and around the world. It starts with you.

Ask yourself these questions, and consider making some reminder notes:

» Next time, how could your expectations be rebalanced to more truly benefit those you visit?

» How could you more fully practice the ministry of presence—in planning your trip agenda and also in your interpersonal interactions within your group's planned activities?

» How might you shift your focus toward learning, connecting, and engaging the underlying issues—preparing yourself to be an effective voice and change agent back home?

» How could you better balance action with deeper reflection each day, both with your group and on your own?

» What satisfaction would you find in being an agent of long-term change for others? What could you do to better understand fundamental challenges and address unjust systems and structures, as well as administer mercy to people negatively affected by those systems and structures?

CREATING A JUST WORLD—IT'S NOT ONLY ABOUT *THEM*

For most of us who are the world's "haves," responding out of sympathy—feeling sorry for the plight of others—comes easy. We quickly recognize the disparity of how we live versus how most of the world lives, and we feel compelled to make some gesture toward restitution, even if only out of guilt. But sympathy is a poor motivator and often leads to poor outcomes, such as creating dependency through guilt-assuaging giveaways that reinforce the have/have-not paradigm and do nothing to empower the disenfranchised.

Spending time with the poor moves us from sympathy to empathy—knowing and understanding someone's needs, sorrows, or challenges. And knowing another person is the necessary precursor to loving them.

Jesus doesn't ask us to focus on helping our neighbor. First and foremost he calls us to love our neighbor, as much as we love ourselves. For where there is love, mutuality is possible, prompting dignity-enhancing acts of mutual caring between friends, between peers—between neighbors.

Love, not guilt, is the critical ingredient for one more challenge we each face: having courage to confront the ways in which we may actually be benefitting from the continued poverty of others and are unwittingly perpetuating that poverty through our daily decisions. This is a painful and touchy topic. Each of us is invited by the Holy Spirit, in the Spirit's own time and method, to explore it. As we do so, we may reexamine various behaviors and values in order to be more conscious of these issues and to help create a more just world.

How you feel prompted to respond will be different from how your spouse or friends may respond. This is unique to you. When Peter asked the resurrected Christ beside the Sea of Galilee what would happen to his fellow disciple John, Jesus replied, "What is that to you? *You* must follow me" (John 21:22, emphasis added).

The list of options is long because the advantages we enjoy are many and diverse, from the low prices we demand for consumer goods, to our nation's foreign policies, to how we handle waste and care for God's creation. My aim is not to highlight some pet issues or actions while excluding others, but simply to encourage you.

When you feel a nudge to consider how your actions affect others around the world and what you might do about it, don't stick your head in the sand. Instead, see these as loving invitations from the Holy Spirit. As you consider these invitations, do so not out of guilt but from a posture of love—love for people such as those you met on your trip and others like them.

It has always been difficult for those who benefit from injustice to envision and actively work toward a more just arrangement. Most people would be in favor of equality and justice if there were no reciprocal cost on those who gain from the world's *in*equality, from its *in*justice—people like me and you. This is partly why I still cringe a bit when I hear the word *justice*. I don't enjoy thinking about it; I don't want the complications and tradeoffs.

But the more I personally know those on the short end of the stick, the more I love them, the more I look to Jesus' example of mutuality and self-denial, then the more I can accept these issues not as guilt inducers but as divine invitations to say yes to the kingdom of God.

Martin Luther King Jr. said it perfectly: "Justice at its best is love correcting everything that stands against love." That's worth pondering. When I think of justice in terms of proactive love correcting those things that are unloving to others, I recognize the invitation to do more in the name of loving my neighbor as myself—*even if* it might mean relinquishing some of my own privileges or the benefits that I enjoy over my global neighbors.

I am a white, male, heterosexual, American Christian in a world where each of these attributes is favored and endowed with special privileges not enjoyed by all. Until I'm willing to face squarely the exclusive privileges I enjoy, I only perpetuate the inequities of life and the injustices that others suffer for my privilege—for these are areas where God's kingdom is not yet fully come. As we truly open ourselves to God regarding our participation in unjust systems, the radical call of the kingdom of God becomes clearer but more uncomfortable to those of us who enjoy advantages we did not personally create but benefit from nonetheless. May love drive us to go where we do not wish to go.

I've taken a dozen or more groups to visit the poorest squatter slums on the hills of Tijuana, Mexico. These slums stand in stark contrast to the luxury real estate surrounding San Diego Harbor that can be seen from those hills, beckoning like some forbidden Land of Oz. Living in southern California is at times emotionally difficult for me, being so close to the separate-and-unequal opportunities on each side of the US-Mexico border wall. Remember generosity? I defined it in chapter three as "the added vulnerability we voluntarily expose ourselves to in order to reduce the vulnerability of others." Don't all the walls we build or live behind exist to reduce our own vulnerability and protect our *own* interests? Instead, what might true generosity, even simple neighborliness, look like?

We are all products of our time and place in history. We are molded, shaped, and truncated by our culture. The tremendous privilege of crosscultural encounters is the opportunity to break through those strictures into a larger world, to see the world more through a God's-eye view.

THE MORE WE CONNECT WITH AND COME TO LOVE THE OTHER, THE LESS THREATENING JUSTICE BECOMES AND THE MORE CREATIVE AND COURAGEOUS WE CAN CHOOSE TO BE.

May we have the creativity and courage to find just solutions to our generation's seemingly unsolvable problems. And as we work together toward that end, to speed its coming and replace our fears with love, we can personally reach over the walls and grasp another's hand, perhaps even dislodging a brick or two in the process.

7

THE KEY TO A LIFE-CHANGING JOURNEY ✈

How can we just go back to worrying about things like the kids' grades, piano lessons, social activities and all the many distractions and "worries" of first-world living? . . . Help!!! I really don't want to miss applying the learning from this trip in a permanent way. I'm impatient to know how God is using us or directing us with the privilege of this unique experience, the relationships and knowledge we've been privy to. God help me not waste it! — CLEO

Many people I speak with believe the issues are so overwhelming that they won't be able to do anything about it. — KAREN

God didn't send me to Central America to make me feel bad, but to make me feel something. He wanted me to find compassion, and use that to change the world for someone. I know I can't change the world for everyone, but that is no excuse to do nothing. — DANA

As mentioned earlier, you won't be finished processing your experience when you finish this book. In fact, your most powerful lessons and greatest treasures may come many months or years from now, long after the journey, when more pieces of life's puzzle become clear.

For me, the most powerful insights often come when I see myself making the same choices that I did before my supposedly life-changing experience—choices based on old cultural habits and paradigms that are at odds with the lessons I *thought* I had learned! As the apostle Paul laments, "I do not understand my own actions. For I do not do what I want, but I do the very thing I hate" (Romans 7:15 NRSV). If my life is to be a tapestry that transcends the monochrome outlook of my home culture, then these discouraging reminders show me the edges of my weaving progress so far.

These are truths I don't like to admit. I'm afraid I might feel guilt. Yet it's just as possible I'll sense a new revelation.

As I write this, I'm sitting on the shores of a lake in North Carolina, thanks to the generosity of some friends who let me use their home as a writing haven. I look down their small dock to a lovely covered platform suspended over the water on stilts. It's a modest eight-by-twelve-foot structure, with sturdy posts and a shingled roof. An inner tube and some fishing equipment lie there, awaiting enjoyment. The lazy water licks up the posts as birds go about their business around me.

My memory suddenly transports me back to homes suspended above the *clong* waterways of Bangkok, Thailand, or tethered to riverbanks in rural Vietnam. These ramshackle versions of the small structure now in front of me might house an entire family, and a drop door inside would provide access to a fish-growing pen or perhaps serve as the family toilet.

In itself, the scene in my mind is simply an unlabeled trip down memory lane; it's not a guilt trip, a pleasure trip, or a learning trip.

I could choose to feel bad about the contrast, sitting here in this idyllic setting—a response I admit I've struggled with many times as I've considered such dissonant scenes. But guilt is not learning.

I could be self-absorbedly grateful that I don't have to live in those difficult circumstances and try to shut off the uncomfortable memory. But this type of thankfulness also shuts off empathy with our human family and our shared world.

The invitation for learning, growth, and integration comes only when I stay in the scene and allow the memory to form itself—when I don't shut it off due to fear or discomfort. And I don't fixate either. Instead, I talk to God: *Thank you for a quiet place where I can reflect. Would you please use this time (or this healthy meal, or the blessing of this quiet place) to strengthen and renew me, so that I can be about the work of your kingdom, mindful of the needs of others, loving mercy, doing justly, and walking humbly with you?*

No one should have to live in deplorable, unsafe housing. Yet I can't magically fix this. But that fact doesn't make the problem less real, and it doesn't make it unfixable. If it is real, then God already knows and cares deeply about it. I want to let my heart be broken by the things that break God's heart, to peacefully trust that the Holy Spirit may be bringing forth the memory, and to embrace Jesus' agenda. So I try to acknowledge and interweave *my* present reality with *their* present reality and remind myself that my life's purpose includes working toward a world in which "never again will there be . . . an infant who lives but a few days" (Isaiah 65:20).

Frankly, if entertainment or leisure or tourism were the driving goals of my life, I don't think I would be able to fend off feelings of guilt when these memories come. Instead, I would probably try hard to push the memories away. I would look for "proofs" from my crosscultural experience in which some apparently inactive people I observed there could be interpreted as hopelessly lazy, where I could blame a people or a government for ineptitude or corruption. I might think about the lovely children standing on those stilt-house porches, who eagerly waved to us with bright smiles, and simply shrug off their deplorable living conditions ("Well, they *looked* happy enough!"). Or I could consider my shoddy unskilled volunteer efforts comparable with the quality of work of humanitarian professionals and write off the latter as bleeding heart do-gooders with little chance of seeing real change take place.

In other words, I would search zealously for evidence that these problems are intractable, the solutions are unworkable, and there's nothing I can do about any of it.

Plenty of travelers do exactly this. They block it out. They write it off. They shrug. In the process, of course, they choose to reinforce the world's status quo over being a force for good, and they forfeit the potential for personal life change—or for using their lives to impact those issues or those children who were so full of potential and goodwill toward all.

Worse, perhaps, in pushing aside the memories they refuse to "remember the poor," the very thing the elders in Jerusalem counseled the apostle Paul to do as their key advice for ensuring his teaching was in line with Jesus (Galatians 2:10).

Here's the point: I didn't *plan* to think about those precarious homes on stilts when I woke up today. I simply gazed out at the boathouse on the lake for the hundredth time, and suddenly the crosscultural memories came flooding back—the similarities, the differences, the dissonance between those living conditions and my own current surroundings.

In a way, there's really only one thing required to start integrating your one-time experiences into your ongoing life: a willingness to embrace memories when they come and to then reflect on them instead of pushing them away. Not much is needed for this process—mainly courage. Because it is our fears that keep us from reflecting—fears of guilt, of ruining the moment, of sadness.

But imagine your spouse or child or parent was a soldier in a distant war. When some special memory of that loved one was triggered as you went about your day, would you block it out? Of course not. You wouldn't be ruining your day to embrace that memory, even if it made you sad or anxious; you would be keeping the home fires burning in your heart for that person. You would be prompted to pray for an end to the conflict and for safety for your loved one. You would act on their behalf—reading and learning more, perhaps volunteering or advocating for their cause, sending letters, gifts, and money.

"Who is my neighbor?" the lawyer asked Jesus, seeking to justify himself. Jesus' answer in his seminal parable of the good Samaritan (Luke 10:25-37) might be interpreted different ways, but clearly, at minimum, *a neighbor includes those God puts in our path*. Through your crosscultural encounters, God has put new people and new situations directly in your path.

It's not morbid to keep your heart burning for those people and issues that have crossed your path; it's Christianity 101.

If we faithfully kindled memories of a loved one in a far-off war, we would sometimes find ourselves with a sense of being in two places at once. And so it is with keeping the flame alive from our crosscultural encounters.

We ourselves become crosscultural.

This means our hearts and minds can move with increasing ease across multiple cultures—we can be "here" and "there" at the same time. We now have friends and heroes in places very different from our own. We can conjure thoughts of *I wonder what she's doing right now?* as readily as we might do so with other loved ones. These thoughts might seem either pleasant or unpleasant at first, but they are available for us to ponder if we have the courage to not avoid them.

Being crosscultural is at times *counter*cultural. We possess more perspectives from which to draw, rather than simply parroting the culture in which we grew up. This means we have the tools to choose differently at times than others around us. We can question our culture's assumptions, expectations, and pressures. We can appreciate all that is good in our own culture while having new eyes to stand back and question other aspects we previously assumed to be a given. We are increasingly able to mix in lessons we've learned from other cultures, creating our own unique (and ever-shifting) blend, reflecting on our experiences without fear, listening to the Spirit, and measuring all of it against Jesus' expectation for citizens—citizens not only of the whole wide world that God created and loves, but of the kingdom of heaven.

YOUR TRIP WAS ONLY THE BEGINNING

I've been like a depressed Charlie Brown character all month since I returned from my mind-transforming trip to Tanzania. I've been wondering, where is joy found at Christmastime? I know for sure it is not found in the mall or even in my sweet, entitled little American offspring. I almost threw a shoe at the TV the other night when I heard the words, "This Christmas, give yourself [fill in the blank]. You deserve it." That made my skin crawl. This Christmas, I don't want the "show." . . . I want the grit of a messy birth in a barn. I want to grasp the magnitude of infinite, inconceivable God entrusting himself as a weak, breakable mortal. I want to wonder.   — BETH

I arise in the morning torn between a desire to improve the world and a desire to enjoy the world. This makes it hard to plan the day.   — E. B. WHITE

National Public Radio ran a story about volunteer tourism, or "voluntourism," that included an interview with a for-profit tour operator from Guatemala. Ken Jones explained that his business has changed significantly over the past two decades. "It used to be beach and beer," Ken says. "And now it's, 'Well, I want to come down and learn something and figure out how to help or be a part of something.' It was more superficial 20 years ago, maybe."

Ken's comment perfectly illustrates the underlying positive trend that supersedes all of the growing pains of this movement of crosscultural caring. On the whole, I'm bullish about the growth of short-term missions and other forms of volunteer tourism. Major societal shifts are always messy, clumsy, and uneven, and sometimes they cause unintended negative effects, which need honest critique and urgent assessment to correct.

Yet you have participated in an important movement, a movement away from self-centered entertainment travel toward service to others and interpersonal connections with the wider world.

In early 1986, I made my first trip to then-communist Ethiopia, which was still reeling from historic drought and famine. We arrived at the airport in Addis Ababa and were driven under a red arch complete with hammer and sickle, past statues of Lenin and the huge parade grounds used for Soviet-style shows of power. The politicized stridency all around us was disconcerting.

We checked into a well-known American hotel chain, a what's-wrong-with-this-picture oasis of capitalism and comfort with sprawling gardens, a lovely pool, and high-quality conveniences. It was also, frankly, a breath of fresh air and a chance to exhale. We were told this was really the only place for Westerners to stay.

I checked into my room and began to relax a bit, then pulled open the curtains. Below, just beyond the walls of the hotel compound, stood a sprawling slum of rusted iron roofs, a hundred Tin Pan Alleys stretching in every direction. The sights, sounds, and smells of urban poverty in developing nations can be very disturbing; even more so here, given the complete disconnect between my hotel room and the reality below.

Perched in my room, safely behind the picture window with the air conditioner running, the disparity between my comfort and their squalor was shocking to me, even though we were there to help. I can only imagine the shock experienced by so many when they check into their luxury beach resort on a pleasure trip in a developing country and see similar sights.

Some quit traveling to those destinations because the disparity is so upsetting. Yet this strikes me as quite a wrong-headed response. The inequality exists, so avoiding it doesn't make it any better. In fact, those economies will actually suffer, and not experiencing the place and people makes it less likely we will do anything about their plight.

Short-term missions and other crosscultural encounters are changing that. It's as though twenty years ago a family took a vacation to a fancy beachside hotel at some exotic locale, and the kids glanced out the window and saw the slums. They watched the local mothers and fathers returning to their darkened hovels at dusk, shoulders slumped. Now those kids are young adults, and they've left the hotel grounds and walked into the slum to say, "What can we do to help?"

Recently, I had coffee with a college graduate who had virtually that experience. She was interested in going to work for a humanitarian organization and was seeking my counsel. She comes from a well-to-do family, and I asked her how she developed her heart for those in need. She answered, "We took a lot of trips when I was growing up, to some exotic places. My parents, especially my mom, always made sure that we took time to see the poor areas nearby. She always made sure we were aware of the disparities and the needs of others."

I commend these parents, as this practice was a way to model empathy and compassion, not to expose their children to poverty simply "so they won't take everything they have for granted." These childhood encounters with cultures very different from her own left an indelible impression on the heart of this young woman and may influence her career decisions. Indeed, every time we travel we have an opportunity to expand our crosscultural understanding.

When have you experienced a similar stark disparity? How did it make you feel? How did you want to respond? What are you angry or passionate about? How can you turn that anger and passion into something useful for others and for the kingdom of God?

In my research for this book, I reviewed a number of compelling articles and surveys that are critical of short-term missions, volunteer tourism, educational trips, and social entrepreneur or "heropreneur" infatuations. All of these critiques are important correctives.

But despite these valid criticisms and my own concerns, I remain optimistic about the future. An estimated $2 billion is now spent annually on over 1.6 million voluntourists of various types. While some of this money and effort might have been spent on more effective ways of helping the poor, persecuted, or marginalized, in truth a far greater portion might have been spent on less meaningful pursuits. Beaches and beer and luxury vacations, for instance.

And, as my story of the recent graduate illustrates, the trip is not the end of the matter. It can be an important beginning, a launching pad to better, more fulfilling life choices. It can lead not only to more compassionate hearts but perhaps to a more just world, something that better reflects Jesus' vision of the reign of God on earth.

And so your *real* journey has only just begun! Ask God what you are to learn about next, what to commit to praying about. Discover a cause that stirs you, and use your crosscultural encounter as a launching pad to do something about it.

God will join you there. And lots of other people might want to as well.

Because a life lived in connection with and in service to others is the only life worthy of the word.

ACKNOWLEDGMENTS

Four years ago, I saw the gaping need that this book attempts to address and felt compelled to do something about it. I invested a week at InterVarsity's Campus by the Sea summer camp working on it, but in the end it was clear the book was not coming together. Yet the stirrings came back a couple years later, and it was because of the encouragement and facilitation of many others that you're now holding this resource.

Part of the genesis for this book must be credited to my mid-career daughter, Karey Sabol. Having spent some fifteen years leading college study-abroad programs at a variety of large and small, private and state universities, we discovered that the same challenges and disappointing realities face these programs as face short-term missions and related trips. As we compared notes, study results, and the utter lack of available resources on what needs to happen *after the trip*, Karey encouraged me, recommended several scholastic-based resources, and was a collaborator on key topics.

My deep appreciation goes out to Bob Putman, Jane Sutton, Carol Stigger, and other writer/editor friends who kindly but firmly encouraged me to embrace the authority of my experience in leading teams and often walking with crosscultural travelers for many subsequent years and to fully "use my voice."

Many thanks to Eric and Mary for providing a wonderfully peaceful setting for much of the writing of this manuscript, and to Steve for connecting us.

Anne Grizzle, Jan Farley, Tom Theriault, Marty Barclay, Bill Reichardt, and several other encouragers kept me going at key points along the way.

I appreciate Brian Fikkert and Steve Corbett of Chalmers Center, Bob Lupton at FCS, and Claire Bennett and Daniela Papi of Learning Service for their important and inspiring writings to help improve various types of short-term volunteer travel. Each of you has attempted to "keep the baby" while throwing out the dirty bathwater.

To the many respondents—both travelers and trip leaders—who submitted heartfelt responses to my surveys and allowed me to quote them.

To Cindy Bunch and the team at InterVarsity Press for believing in this project and assigning Rebecca Carhart as my editor and a helpful team of colleagues to bring this book to fruition.

Finally, to my wife, Janet, who believed in this project and believes in me. She has given me the gift of time to pour all of myself that was necessary for this book to come to fruition and has been my most frequent editor and partner. Her love and support is my constant joy.

What Now?

1. Studies of short mission trips and college service-learning experiences show that there is virtually no lasting change in the lives of the travelers. Why do you think this is?

2. How do you feel about the concept of integration, interweaving, or threading? What advantages do you see to living an integrated or interwoven life?

3. What apprehensions do you have around integrating other cultural viewpoints and values into your life? Discuss these with others if possible.

Coming Home with Gifts

1. How does the idea that you come home bearing gifts for yourself deepen your appreciation for the experiences you had and the value of reflecting on those?

2. Have you struggled to answer the question, "How was your trip?" Why?

3. Does the author's view of life change make you feel more pressure or less pressure? Why?

4. If "there is a stewardship required from the experiences we've been given," what ideas do you have about how you can be a good steward (or responsible caretaker) of your experiences?

5. Did a "picture-window" story from your crosscultural experience come to mind as you read? How might telling such a story provide you with a more satisfying response to the question, "How was your trip?"

6. Try writing or telling your own picture-window story. What details should you put in and what distractions can you leave out? (Don't worry about perfection—the point is to tell one story, preferably from a human encounter.)

7. What unpleasant feelings have you had—whether during or after your trip—that surprised you? What do you think these feelings were in response to?

   We can't constructively address what we can't admit or even name. Try reading slowly the following list of feelings many people have experienced, and take a breath with each one to consider whether it applies to you: *Guilt. Disappointment. Discouragement. Overwhelmed. Disgust. Jealousy. Exhaustion. Threatened. Judgment. Prejudice. Phony. Inadequate.* Write or talk with someone to unpack any that resonate with you.

Mining for Gold

1. Contemplative theologian Richard Rohr writes that "it is a risky position to live undefended, in a kind of constant openness to the other," yet he also claims that "Spirit-led people never stop growing and changing." What does "living undefended" mean to you? How does this openness feel risky?

2. How might your crosscultural experience open you to new ways of reading Scripture?

3. What is the problem with telling stories from your trip in a way that puts the spotlight on you?

4. What lessons are you gleaning from your trip that can be applied to "unplanned" crosscultural encounters in your everyday life?

5. During your trip, did you or your travelmates declare something was "good" or "bad" only to discover a nuanced reality later? What insights or practices would you need to employ in order to paint a more realistic—and fair—picture of cultural realities you encounter?

6. It could be said that gratitude is an excellent place to start and a terrible place to stop. How can you embrace gratitude while not stopping there?

7. Since your trip, how do you think differently about the question, "Who is my neighbor?"

Treasures on the Journey

1. What examples of our shared humanity did you experience on your trip? Did any surprise you?

2. In what scenarios would you agree with Fr. Greg Boyle's assertion that "It's not *us versus them*; there is only us"? Where might you disagree? How have your views shifted in this regard in light of your crosscultural encounters?

3. How did you experience generosity during your crosscultural trip?

4. How do you react to the author's statement that "generosity could be measured as the added vulnerability we voluntarily

expose ourselves to in order to reduce the vulnerability of others"?

5. What other treasures are you uncovering from your own crosscultural journey?

Keeping the Lines Open

1. Two years from now, how would you like to answer this question: *How did my crosscultural experience lead to tangible positive change, both for me and for the people and communities I met?*

2. What are some ways you've felt powerless to do anything about an important issue facing people you met on your trip? How could you take meaningful action now by learning more, advocating, connecting, or using your voice?

3. Read Joanna Macy's quote again (pp. 73-74). How could realizing that apathy and disconnection come mainly from our fear of pain become a "pivot point" in our own lives? How should we observe and respond to our fears?

4. Have you fostered any ongoing connections with those you met or with the issues and challenges they and their culture face? If not, how could you connect in a meaningful way?

5. Have you banded together with others concerning an issue or need from the culture you visited? What is one next step you could take in this regard?

6. Proverbs 31:8 says, "Speak up for those who cannot speak for themselves." In what settings might you have opportunities to speak up?

7. What barriers have kept or might keep you from speaking up on behalf of others?

8. How would you describe your personal sphere of influence? How did Mark and Jennifer's story make you think about the value of sharing your personal stories in your own sphere of influence?

Make Your Next Trip Your Best Trip

1. How have your personal goals or expectations for crosscultural experiences inadvertently been at odds with truly helping those you came to serve? What personal goals and expectations would be more constructive?

2. What did you think about the concept of learning service instead of service learning, and how might you apply it to your next crosscultural experience?

3. How might the idea of "the ministry of presence" shift your focus—and your schedule—on your next trip?

4. Looking back on your last trip and ahead toward any future ones, what have you learned about reflection and debriefing habits that you want to continue? What would you like to change or add?

5. How have your past crosscultural experiences helped you grow in exercising mercy?

6. In current and future ministry opportunities, how might you widen your focus to also explore issues of injustice?

7. What made you feel uncomfortable in this section? What spurred you to openness? How is Martin Luther King's idea

that "justice at its best is love correcting everything that stands against love" an invitation to a more motivating way to look at these issues?

8. Review the summary principles in "Pondering and Planning Your Next Crosscultural Encounter" (p. 105). Which seem the most important to address on your next trip? What could you do to improve future trips that you or your church, school, or organization take?

The Key to a Life-Changing Journey

1. Since returning, have you had memories of your crosscultural experience come flooding back in the midst of your everyday life? What did you do with those?

2. Why might it take courage to embrace memories of your trip when they come?

3. How does the analogy of having a loved one in a distant war speak to you? How might you similarly "keep the home fires burning" for those you visited in a different culture?

4. What are your top three takeaways from this book?

5. What are the top three practices or actions you'd like to begin next?

Appendix

For further reflection, here is a summary version of Dr. Tim Dearborn's excellent Eight Great Questions, adapted with permission from *Short-Term Missions Workbook*, rev. ed. (Downers Grove, IL: InterVarsity Press, 2018). Tim's book includes more in-depth expansions of each question.

1. **Who am I?**

   What have I learned about myself?

2. **Who is God?**

   How has my understanding of God changed?

3. **Who are we?**

   What have I learned about community?

4. **What is the impact of culture on faith?**

   How do I see life and the gospel (the good news of the kingdom of God) differently because of what I've experienced?

5. **What's wrong with the world?**

   Why is there such suffering and injustice in it?

6. **What does it mean to be a follower of Christ?**

   What have I learned about discipleship?

7. **What's of value?**

How do I live here in light of what I've seen there?

8. **Where am I going?**

What is God calling me to be and to do as a result of this experience?

NOTES

1 What Now?

4   *studies have almost universally found*: See Kurt Alan Ver Beek's excellent roundup of the most relevant studies: "Lessons from the Sapling: Review of Quantitative Research on Short-Term Missions," in *Effective Engagement in Short-Term Missions: Doing It Right!*, ed. Robert J. Priest, Kindle ed. (Pasadena, CA: William Carey Library, 2008). Ver Beek concludes that "participants did have a very positive experience and intended that the experience would translate into action—*but most often it did not*" (chap. 17; emphasis added).

6   *Peace Corps handbook*: Peace Corps, "RPCV Handbook: You're on Your Way Home," 10, http://files.peacecorps.gov/resources/returned /staycon/rpcv_handbook.pdf.

7   *my own attempts*: The collection of meditations in Cory Trenda, *Reflections from Afar: Unexpected Blessings for Those Who "Have" from Those Who Don't* (World Vision Resources, 2010) may provide additional fodder for your ongoing processing. See also the "Eight Great Questions" in Tim Dearborn, *Short-Term Missions Workbook*, rev. ed. (Downers Grove, IL: InterVarsity Press, 2018).

2 Coming Home with Gifts

17   *It is precisely through*: Frederick Buechner, *Telling Secrets* (New York: HarperCollins, 1991), 30.

22   *In one sentence tell them*: For a helpful tool on sorting out your most meaningful encounters, see Steve Moore's "Telling Your Story" worksheet, adapted from Moore, *Living for the Long Haul: A Debriefing Manual for Short-Term Missionaries*, 1996; reprinted in *Missions Catalyst*, June 24, 2009, http://missionscatalyst.net /wp-content/uploads/2010/05/Telling-Your-Story.pdf.

35   *You might consider changing up*: A few devotional-style resources that
     I and others have found especially meaningful include *Finding Cal-
     cutta: What Mother Teresa Taught Me About Meaningful Work and
     Service*, by Mary Poplin; *Theirs Is the Kingdom: Celebrating the Gospel
     in Urban America*, by Robert D. Lupton; *Traveling Hopefully, Reflec-
     tions for Pilgrims in the Fast Lane*, by Stan Mooneyham; and my col-
     lection of meditations, *Reflections from Afar: Unexpected Blessings
     for Those Who "Have" from Those Who Don't*, by Cory Trenda.

3 Mining for Gold

40   *scripture's consistent portrayal*: Wesley Granberg-Michaelson, "An
     Anchor in the Storm," *Sojourners*, April 2017, https://sojo.net
     magazine/april-2017/anchor-storm.

41   *In my experience*: Richard Rohr, "Vulnerability," Daily Meditations,
     Center for Action and Contemplation, September 27, 2016, https://
     cac.org/vulnerability-2016-09-27.

45   *Tera*: A pseudonym.

54   *No longer do I feel guilty*: Peter Greer and David Weekley, *The Giver
     and the Gift: Principles of Kingdom Fundraising* (Minneapolis:
     Bethany House, 2015), 63.

54   *is not only the greatest*: M. Tullius Cicero, *For Plancius* 80, in *The
     Orations of Marcus Tullius Cicero*, trans. C. D. Yonge and B. A.
     London (George Bell & Sons, 1891).

4 Treasures on the Journey

57   *I've gleaned many precious gems*: See my book *Reflections from Afar:
     Unexpected Blessings for Those Who "Have" from Those Who Don't*
     for more of my own attempts at processing and integrating.

58   *I note the obvious differences*: Maya Angelou, "Human Family," in *I
     Shall Not Be Moved* (New York: Random House, 1990), 5.

59   *It's not us versus them*: See Greg Boyle, "There Is No Us and Them,
     Only Us," March 7, 2014, www.youtube.com/watch?v=CDKDekAeabU.

5 Keeping the Lines Open

69   *how would you like to answer*: Thanks to Steve Corbett and Brian
     Fikkert in *Helping Without Hurting in Short-Term Missions* (Chicago:
     Moody Publishers, 2014) for articulating this idea.

70   *Bodai*: A pseudonym.

73   *Apathy and denial stem*: "Joanna Macy: A Wild Love for the World,"
     interview with Krista Tippett, *On Being*, August 11, 2016.

83   *If you watched a movie*: Donald Miller, *A Million Miles in a Thousand
     Years: How I Learned to Live a Better Story* (Nashville: Thomas
     Nelson, 2009), xiii.

6 Make Your Next Trip Your Best Trip

85   *the most common shortcomings*: For more on potential problems as-
     sociated with "voluntourism," see Michelle L. Staton, "7 Reasons
     Why Your Two Week Trip To Haiti Doesn't Matter: Calling Bull on
     'Service Trips' and Voluntourism," The Almost Doctor's Channel,
     December 15, 2015, http://almost.thedoctorschannel.com/14323-2,
     and the list of resources at the end of the article.

85   *Recent important books*: Steve Corbett and Brian Fikkert, *When
     Helping Hurts: How to Alleviate Poverty Without Hurting the Poor . . .
     and Yourself*; Steve Corbett and Brian Fikkert, *Helping Without
     Hurting in Short-Term Missions*; Robert D. Lupton, *Toxic Charity: How
     Churches and Charities Hurt Those They Help (And How to Reverse It)*.

87   *Such experiences have been critiqued*: As one example of many, see
     Daniela Papi, "What's Wrong with Volunteer Travel?," TEDx Ox-
     bridge, June 30, 2013, www.youtube.com/watch?v=oYWl6Wz2NB8.

88   *Learning Service*: See www.learningservice.info.

88   *As they contend*: Claire Bennett and Daniela Papi, "From Service
     Learning to Learning Service," *Stanford Social Innovation Review*,
     April 8, 2014, https://ssir.org/articles/entry/from_service_learning
     _to_learning_service.

89 *alleviating poverty*: Richard Stearns, "Solving Poverty Is Rocket Science," *Christianity Today*, July 8, 2013, www.christianitytoday.com/ct/2013/july-web-only/solving-poverty-is-rocket-science.html.

89 *the percentage of the global population*: See the World Bank's Global Monitoring Report 2015/2016 for details, including the fact that extreme poverty has been more than cut in half since 1990. World Bank Group, *Development Goals in an Era of Demographic Change* (Washington, DC: World Bank, 2016), http://pubdocs.worldbank.org/en/503001444058224597/Global-Monitoring-Report-2015.pdf.

93 *On one trip to the Afar region*: This story is adapted from "The Ministry of Touch, Tears and Blood" and "Hungry Hearts" in Cory Trenda, *Reflections from Afar: Unexpected Blessings for Those Who "Have" from Those Who Don't* (World Vision Resources, 2010).

95 *In healing*: Stan Mooneyham, *Traveling Hopefully: Reflections for Pilgrims in the Fast Lane* (Waco, TX: Word, 1984), 39.

98 *Psychologists point out*: For more on this, read some of the many resources on Transformative Learning Theory. A recent scholarly review of studies on Transformative Learning Theory and the impact of mission trips on participants is Brian Bain, "The Impact of Short-Term Missions on the Long-Term Missional Development of Participants" (PhD diss., Fuller Theological Seminary, School of Intercultural Studies, 2015).

103 *much has been written recently about orphanage homes*: See the websites for the ChildSafe Movement (www.thinkchildsafe.org) and Tourism Concern (www.tourismconcern.org.uk), and a growing number of articles and studies, including UNICEF's *With the Best Intentions: A Study of Attitudes Toward Residual Care in Cambodia*, 2011, www.unicef.org/eapro/Study_Attitudes_towards_RC.pdf.

107 *Justice at its best*: Martin Luther King Jr., *The Autobiography of Martin Luther King Jr.*, ed. Clayborne Carson (New York: Warner Books, 1998), 325.

7 The Key to a Life-Changing Journey

116   *National Public Radio ran a story*: Carrie Kahn, "As 'Voluntourism' Explodes in Popularity, Who's It Helping Most?," *Goats and Soda* (blog), NPR, July 31, 2014, www.npr.org/sections/goatsandsoda /2014/07/31/336600290.

119   *Indeed, every time we travel*: In *Travel as a Political Act* (Berkeley, CA: Avalon, 2014), travel guide Rick Steves also extols the options we create by choosing to be "travelers" instead of simply "tourists."